Under Cover

First Edition published in Canada and United States
Published by Optimum Publishing International.

LIBRARY AND ARCHIVES CANADA CATALOGUING IN PUBLICATION
Title: Under Cover, Inside the Shady World
of Organized Crime and the RCMP
Garry Clement.

Subjects: Espionage, Organized Crime, Policing, Chinese Triads, RCMP, Money Laundering
Description: Optimum Publishing International Canada edition

ISBN 978-0-88890-344-0 (Trade Paperback)
ISBN 978-0-88890- 352-5 (ePub)

Book design by Jessica Albert

PRINTED AND BOUND IN CANADA
Marquis Printing

For information on rights or any submissions, please e-mail to
Optimum: deanb@opibooks.com
Optimum Publishing International
Dean Baxendale, President & CEO
Toronto, Canada

www.optimumpublishinginternational.com
www.opibooks.com
Twitter @opibooks | Instagram @opibooks

OPTIMUM
PUBLISHING
INTERNATIONAL
LONDON I MONTRÉAL I TORONTO

What People Are Saying...

"Intriguing and revealing . . . A dedicated police officers's enduring search for the truth!"

> — **DAVID CASSELS**, President, Coalition for Canadian Police Reform

"Garry Clement is a national treasure. He's spent his life in service to Canada and I guarantee he knows more about international organized crime, drug trafficking, money laundering and the state actors—China, Iran, Mexico, Russia—who today pose a major national security threat to Canada. This book should be required reading by every politician and bureaucrat in Ottawa, and everyone else who cares about the future of this country."

> — **JEFFREY ROBINSON**, bestselling author of *The Laundrymen*, *The Merger*, and *The Sink*

"This book provides incredible operational details of the complex organized and financial crime cases Garry Clement has worked on over his decades-long remarkable career with the RCMP and beyond. It also includes fascinating information regarding his critically important leadership work in both the anti-terrorism and counter-espionage sectors. In addition, the book details his telling insights into the operational, institutional and systemic issues he gained throughout his career, which is essential to reforms that remain necessary today. If these issues are relevant to you, and they should be, this book is a must-read."

> — **SCOTT NEWARK** LLB

Under Cover

INSIDE THE SHADY WORLD OF ORGANIZED CRIME AND THE RCMP

GARRY CLEMENT

OPTIMUM
PUBLISHING
INTERNATIONAL
LONDON I MONTRÉAL I TORONTO

Contents

Dedication

I dedicate this book to my wife, Lee, and my daughters, Melissa and Nicole. They stood with me throughout my career, even under the most trying circumstances. I could not have asked for or received more phenomenal support, and for this I am eternally grateful.

My career would have been unsuccessful had it not been for the many dedicated officers who worked with me and bought into my vision. There are far too many to name, but they all know who they are. Canada is a much safer place due to their commitment over the years.

Author's Note

What follows is an overview of my policing career. Most of the names mentioned are real, but in a few cases I have opted to use first names only, as those individuals at the time of the offence were quite young and have now served their sentence.

I have been as factual as I was able without getting into areas that would still be classified as secret, but those areas are limited. My intent is not to negate the RCMP's value but to show that the organization is in need of total cultural change.

Introduction

by Christian Leuprecht, PhD

As a scholar seized with the impact of organized and financial crime on Canada, I became aware of Garry Clement through his online and public engagement on this matter. He is widely regarded for his reputation, professionalism and leadership on this file. For over a decade, I have witnessed Garry's commitment to improving Canada's record to thwart money laundering and transnational organized crime. Garry's extensive track record as a consultant on policing and financial crime gives him exemplary credibility and experience to advise government and decision-makers on matters of public policy and administration for Canada to meet its public safety and national security priorities on financial crime, as well as the international obligations to which it has signed on but long neglected.

In 2021, I was invited to assemble a dream team of the country's best minds and seasoned professionals to provide expert witness testimony on containing financial crime before the Cullen Commission on Money Laundering in British Columbia. Garry was the obvious choice as the team's law enforcement professional: articulate, well-known, and a highly regarded expert on financial crime in general and Asian-based organized crime in particular. Garry's undercover experience had given him a firsthand understanding of how organized crime functions in Canada. In addition, his posting as the RCMP Liaison Officer to the Canadian Consulate General in Hong Kong from 1991 to 1994 afforded him firsthand insights into Asian-based organized crime, their relationship with China and its harmful impact on community safety in Canada.

As a popular speaker at many financial crime conferences throughout North America and a go-to expert for the national media, I have come to appreciate his honesty and objectivity, along with his uncanny ability to explain financial crime straightforwardly. When I assembled a team of contributors to a volume on the topic, one former official stood out as the obvious choice to write from the federal law enforcement perspective: Garry. In September 2023, McGill-Queen's University Press published *Dirty Money: Financial Crime in Canada* as part of the longstanding Canada: State of the Federation series. The book's aim aligns perfectly with Garry's: to raise the level of informed debate by making as complex and obtuse a subject as financial crime and its consequences accessible to the broader public, politicians and law enforcement.

Garry has so much to offer, and I commend him for putting great effort into assembling his wisdom and experience in his own book. It is a labour of love that I am honoured and delighted to endorse as a milestone contribution to a public debate on policing and financial crime. His outstanding monograph is mandatory for anyone looking to get up to speed and make common cause on this critical subject.

CHRISTIAN LEUPRECHT, PhD
Kingston, October 2023

Foreword

by Vern White

Under Cover offers readers a front-row seat to the gritty realities of the criminal underworld, providing a rare and intimate glimpse into the clandestine operations that challenge law enforcement. The narrative, presented from a first-person perspective, allows readers to step into the shoes of those on the front lines, experiencing the adrenaline-pumping highs and the gut-wrenching lows that come with battling organized crime.

The author's storytelling abilities weave together a tapestry of experiences, blending research with personal anecdotes. Not only does the book delve into the operations and intricacies of criminal enterprises, but it also humanizes the struggle faced by law enforcement personnel. The author unravels the personal challenges encountered while combating criminal elements, shedding light on the toll it can take both professionally and personally. The author brings the work of a criminal investigator combating organized crime together with his small "p" political challenges inside Canada's national police force, the Royal Canadian Mounted Police.

In addition to highlighting the operational challenges, the book doesn't shy away from shedding light on the personal dynamics within a law enforcement agency, offering readers a glimpse into the bureaucratic hurdles that can complicate the fight against organized crime. This unvarnished perspective underscores the multifaceted battle that law enforcement must navigate to uphold justice and ensure the safety of communities.

The book's detailed narratives provide a deeper understanding of the complexities inherent in dismantling criminal networks. It underscores the need for a multifaceted approach, intertwining tactical expertise, strategic coordination, and relentless determination. Through this riveting storytelling, readers are given a chance to see from the front row the dedication and sacrifices required to maintain the integrity of a nation facing the pervasive influence of organized crime.

Under Cover is an essential read for those wanting exposure to the pervasive impact of organized crime on Canadian society. It can serve as a wake-up call, urging society to be proactive in the fight against crime, promoting collaboration between law enforcement and the public to secure a safer and more resilient future.

I enjoyed the read from cover to cover and believe those in society will enjoy it as much as those engaged in law enforcement in Canada.

Preface

The Royal Canadian Mounted Police is no longer fit for purpose. My third death threat really made me understand this sad truth.

On a cold November night in 1981, my wife, Lee, and I had just taken possession of our new home in North Gower, Ontario. I had transferred from the Vancouver Drug Section to the RCMP Headquarters in Ottawa. We, along with my sister, Brenda, were in the process of unpacking boxes. Fortunately for us, we had made arrangements to coincide with our possession date, and our phone was hooked up.

As we were unpacking, the phone rang. On the other end was Corporal Hugh Stewart, whom I had the utmost respect for and recognized as a cop's cop. He directed me to arm myself immediately, take my family to the nearest Ontario Provincial Police detachment, and call him once I arrived at the OPP office. Knowing Hugh as I did, I could tell by his tone he was not joking—something had occurred whose peril seemed imminent.

This was the third threat of its kind that had occurred in my career, and it was one that sounded serious. A lot of thoughts go through your mind in such a position, and this time especially, seeing as I was once again involving my wife and now my sister in a potentially dangerous situation. I am sure most readers have seen movies involving witness protection. You may have seen onscreen what it's like when the individual's location is uncovered by the criminal group they testified against, resulting in fear and a need for immediate action to protect the family. At that exact instance, this was my reality, like something from one of those movies. My first reaction was, *You have to be joking!* Then came the fear and guilt due to what I was putting my loved ones through, especially after moving across the country to avoid such an event! Finally, muscle memory kicked in based on my training, and I reacted.

I vividly recall going next door to my new neighbour and asking them to contact the police if they saw any suspicious activity. I should have realized the impact this would have on them, seeing that I did not offer a lot of explanation. I later learned they barely slept for several nights.

To this day I still remember driving to the OPP detachment in Bells Corners in Ottawa with my wife and sister and a loaded shotgun. I was suspicious of every vehicle that came near us. Could they be a potential threat? Calling Hugh from the OPP office only heightened my concern. I was told they had a source who'd provided information alleging that Eddie Cheese and a couple other associates I'd been instrumental in having arrested had taken out a contract on me, and two hit men from Montreal had agreed to carry it out.

As I look back on this episode, it really demonstrates a circumstance when the RCMP failed to take responsible actions. No local authorities contacted me until the following morning, after I'd already booked myself and my family into a motel in Bells Corners. Common sense should have demanded immediate protection, which would have allayed a lot of stress and safety concerns.

At this time, I also came to realize that there were no operational policies in place that addressed how to handle a threat against a member of the police force. There was no mental health support. Additionally, my family's loss of income was not recognized; Lee had had to give up her job immediately, like *now*, and she'd been escorted out with protection. It had a major impact on her—you can imagine how destabilizing that was. This was a gap that I vowed to resolve when the opportunity afforded itself once I took up my new position as reviewer analyst at the drug enforcement branch in Headquarters in Ottawa. At the same time, I felt close to leaving the force as I was extremely disillusioned in view of how the threat was mismanaged.

During this period in the force's history, it was considered a weakness to give the impression that something such as a threat on your life could negatively affect your health. The standard line of "Suck it up, princess" won the day. And yet, a death threat makes you reflect on your life choices and what brought you to this point. The threats I received, and other pivotal moments that called for reflection, led me to think deeply about my time in the force. Ultimately, among many other considerations, these threats contributed to my choice to retire in 2003. I resolved to get a university degree and endeavoured to get the force to focus on organized crime.

Over the past decade I have been encouraged to write a book by individuals whom I have a lot of respect for: Victor Malarek, Jeffrey Robinson, Julian Sher, Fabian Dawson, Sam Cooper, and Declan Hill, all respected journalists and individuals I am delighted to call professional friends.

I began writing many times but always found a reason to postpone. Other than a few war stories, I did not feel I really had anything to share. My hope is that in some small way this book and my career account will allow me to share many thoughts and opinions about the force I dedicated thirty years to, and that the messaging will represent many other current and former members who go above and beyond and do not simply seek promotion.

What will become evident as you read is that I was not a conformist and often found myself on the outside of the culture that was so prevalent in the RCMP. That being said, I was proud to be able to recommend promotion to many colleagues under my command both from within and from partner organizations who went on to achieve senior management positions and contribute immensely to policing in Canada.

The timing has been perfect for dedicating time to completing this book as I, like many in North America, have been honouring the requirements of COVID restrictions. Recently, finishing the entire series of *Narcos* and *Narcos: Mexico* has also motivated me to complete this endeavour. I feel that we as Canadians do not do a great job of celebrating achievement and dedication in law enforcement as compared to our American counterparts. People like Robert Mazur, a former FBI undercover agent, are celebrated for what they achieve, but here in Canada we give the impression that we have nothing that compares to the investigative prowess of our American colleagues. In fact, we have many officers who have risked their lives and infiltrated organized crime in Canada but have not shared their stories.

I still work as a compliance officer and continue to liaise on money laundering and financial-crime matters. My hope is that before I fully retire and with all the controversies that have occurred and are occurring in the RCMP, my candid overview of life as an RCMP member will encourage our political masters to take definitive action so that we can have an effective and efficient federal investigative force for Canada. This is not meant to detract from many officers who, over the years, put their lives on the line well beyond what is considered general police work. Many of these officers were changed (in some cases, developing stress disorders and addictions) as a result of this work, resulting in stalled careers. Working organized-crime investigations and undercover tends to make a person more outspoken and less adherent to the norm of an obedient and humble servant, a primary reason being that we are exposed to constant stress for long periods of time.

As the majority of the force's members hail from contract policing in uniform, which has its own culture, and one which is far more paramilitary, it is no wonder that many of the commissioned officers (meaning: any officers in management above the rank of sergeant major) are from contract (uniform) policing rather than from investigative policing. Given that the RCMP is a federal institution, its bilingual requirement further negates many highly qualified federal investigative officers from ever reaching the most senior ranks. An understanding of the need for more stringent federal investigative requirements is therefore often overlooked.

I would also argue that the lack of mental health support resulted in many officers quietly and secretly suffering from post-traumatic stress disorder (PTSD). Today this issue is front and centre of cultural awareness within policing, but it did not become a factor until after my tenure. Drinking was often the outlet of choice for many officers. In many cases, their drinking was known to be a problem by management but kept hidden. It has taken me over forty-five years to admit that this has been a challenge for most of my working life.

Undercover in Vancouver, I witnessed the reality of the streets and had the benefit of getting to know two young women who were addicted to heroin. Those experiences fortified my belief that arresting street addicts was a failure of the system. To have any chance of achieving a modicum of success, we need to focus on organized crime, who are the real beneficiaries of drug trafficking—and a blight on society. I also realized that addiction calls for intervention. My view is that the "safe supply" program, which provides free substitute drugs, is a failure, and the only recourse is to have addiction rehab centres with appropriate professionals as part of any public strategy.[1]

Over the course of my career, I also witnessed blatant and wilful ignorance by a few senior leaders. I highlight concrete examples later in this book, but suffice to say it enabled me to formulate the strong opinion that Canada needs an independent commission against corruption as well as stronger protection for whistleblowers. Canada has some of the weakest protections of the G20.

I hope this book will serve to bring awareness and insight to the erosion that exists in federal policing and to demonstrate how the majority of executive RCMP members continue to put contract (uniform) policing ahead of its true mandate: federal law enforcement. These concerns have resulted in the RCMP no longer being fit for its purpose, which has led to the expansion of transnational organized crime in Canada and beyond its borders.

Long before retirement and more so lately I have been a candid spokesperson for policing issues, money-laundering issues, and organized-crime issues through many media outlets. I am sure many former senior RCMP officials see my actions in a negative light, but I believe law enforcement has become far too politicized and is therefore no longer serving the community objectively. I feel that putting down an honest and true perspective of a story serves the greater good. Over the course of my career, I witnessed the politicization that occurred in the force; I saw how senior managers and aspiring senior managers were more concerned about their next promotions than effective policing.

I am sure some of my past colleagues will see this book as coming from a disgruntled former member. But I would do my career over again in a heartbeat. I am still a proud ex-member of the RCMP, notwithstanding the negatives that exist and existed.

A *National Post* article written by David Cassels in 2020 sums up policing today, showing how there is a need for change and a rethinking of policing in Canada.

> Policing is first and foremost a service to the community; the more it is at odds with the needs and values of the community, the less it works.

While these words may be good common sense to most people, the reality is that the police are most often at odds with the needs of the community. This is not the fault of police officers; it is outdated, organizational components that inhibit well-intentioned police from doing their work. Police agencies in Canada are bureaucratic, centralized, impersonal, process oriented, and law-enforcement based. Components are random patrol, rapid response, and investigation after the fact. This is simply the way it is. All empirical studies of police operations have shown that random patrol has no effect on the prevention of crime, victimization, or perception of police effectiveness.

Rapid response by police is marginally effective and in the majority of cases, comes during or after a crime has been committed, leaving the police to spend many hours investigating.

Empirical studies show no evidence that rapid response increases apprehension rates or has any effect on crime rates.

Investigation after the fact is exceptionally time-consuming and has no effect on the reduction of crime.

Police officers are skilled, well-equipped, and committed to their work. They are there when you need them and act immediately to bring some calm to a difficult situation. However, your police have both the ability and opportunity to do much more. It is outdated strategies that impede them from doing so.[2]

Part One

YOUNG GARRY

Chapter One

MY UPBRINGING IN HENSALL, A SMALL RURAL ONTARIO TOWN

Whether a person is born into a profession or if it is our early-life experiences that drive us to a particular career path, I am not sure, but somehow, I can't help believing that I was preordained to be a cop. Growing up in small-town Ontario just north of London, I had a rather ordinary upbringing for a struggling middle-class family. My parents, both of whom worked to provide for my three brothers, one sister, and myself, imbued me from an early age with their Protestant work ethic. Sometime in my formative years I acquired the nickname "Spade"—short for Sam Spade—the fictional private detective and the protagonist of Dashiell Hammett's 1930 novel *The Maltese Falcon*. My father continually accused me of interrogating anyone I came across. He even claimed I learned to talk before I could walk.

My upbringing was mostly uneventful, but due to my girth, I probably looked more like a young Perry Mason than I did a potential law-enforcement officer. I am sure had I been born in the computer age, I would have been one of the many youths today who sit in front of game screens for hours at a time. Yes, I was a robust child who had to wear "huskies." As the second of five children, overweight, with a terrible acne problem as a teenager, and not being mechanically inclined (with a father who owned a machinery business), I developed a real sense of insecurity. This, along with witnessing my father being treated poorly by colleagues of higher status after he took a position with a manufacturer, influenced how I would handle myself throughout my life. I am continually trying to prove myself and I do not suffer fools (a fact that was occasionally an irritant to others in the force). I often use humour to deflect and mask what I am really thinking and feeling, something that has helped me thus far.

The wall next to my childhood bed was covered with RCMP postcards. I am not sure if it was the uniform or my love of *The Hardy Boys* that inspired this focus on the RCMP, but for whatever reason, I was clearly drawn to this profession from an early age.

Fortunately, my reflexes were above average, so I was an average hockey player as long as I stuck to being a goaltender. Like in many small towns in Ontario, hockey was a rite of passage and an integral part of growing up. Our arena was the centre of winter activity for hockey and skating and a place where friendships were forged.

Coming from a working-class family, I had several part-time jobs throughout my childhood and early-teen years, from grass-cutting, assisting the local farms with baling and stacking hay, working in an ice-cream and hamburger shack, and working for an electrician. What I learned on these jobs would prove to be of tremendous value to my policing career.

Hensall was a town where everyone subscribed to the view that it takes a village to raise a child. Regardless of where we were, we were expected to be on good behaviour, or someone, and likely *not* our parents, would take appropriate action.

My father owned a farm-machinery business, which enabled my eldest brother, Ron, and I to learn to drive at a very early age; first we drove tractors, later a small motorcycle, and finally, *real* vehicles.

We even had a small motorcycle club we called "Hensall's Angels," made up of about five kids all under the age of sixteen. Our 50cc and 65cc Hondas allowed us to tour the countryside with virtual impunity. Or at least, so we thought. We were all envious when one of our friends obtained a 250cc Harley Sprint, and we relished the opportunity to drive this *real* motorcycle. On a weekend my parents were away, I opted to take my turn on the Harley. Although the new helmet law was in effect, I wanted to be like "Easy Rider" and took off into the countryside. On my return I found myself explaining to an OPP district inspector why I should not be arrested and taken to juvenile detention. This event stayed with me throughout my career. The officer told me I would be required to appear in court and that I needed to explain the circumstances to my parents, which, upon their return, I promptly did. When the officer found out that I had indeed briefed my parents, as instructed, he chose not to charge me. In doing so, he taught me the value of discretion. I tried to emulate that officer's discernment throughout my career with deserving individuals.

My youngest brother, Bob, initially followed in my footsteps: he also became a goaltender and showed a propensity for good grades in school. His love of transport trucks, however, drew him out of school at a relatively early age. He built a very successful trucking company, which on the surface may not seem relevant, but it was his understanding of trucking and bringing goods into Canada from the United States that was one of the major factors leading to the triumph of my last undercover operation. My relationship with Bob served to legitimize my persona: owner of a trucking company.

I also must credit my eldest brother, Ron, who always looked out for me. He was far too generous with his vehicles, something that I openly admit taking advantage of. Ron always had cars that were the envy of his peers. For me, having the option to borrow everything from Formula 400 Firebirds to four-speed 396 Novas (we called them "four on the floor") while learning how to drive in Ontario's many varying weather conditions made for a great teenage experience.

The year we moved to Elmira, Ontario—1970—was also the year Canada's voting age was lowered from twenty-one to eighteen. Thanks to my phenomenal history teacher Robert Huschka, a man who pushed us to engage in politics and whom I had the greatest respect for, I was selected to travel with Mitchell Sharp. Mr. Sharp treated me like royalty and afforded me the opportunity to meet the Right Honourable Pierre Elliott Trudeau. I must confess, though— as diehard Conservatives, my grandfather and father came close to disowning me for travelling with the Liberals.

During this period, I got involved in a youth group with an anti–drug use focus. Although I'd seldom heard about drug use in Hensall or at my high school in Exeter, Ontario, Elmira was a different story. LSD was in vogue, as was marijuana. For some reason, I took a firm position against drugs from the outset and formed the view that I was going to get into policing and become a drug officer. I naïvely thought I could save the world.

Grade 13 solidified my resolve to join the RCMP. In my final semester I submitted my application to the Kitchener office. The rest is history. The strong views I developed as a youth stuck with me throughout my career. My goal was to become the best police officer I could, with a focus on drug enforcement and organized crime.

Chapter Two

RCMP ENLISTMENT AND DEPOT TRAINING

On May 3, 1973, I was sworn in to the RCMP at 225 Jarvis Street in Toronto, the RCMP headquarters for Ontario, along with Henry Wamsteeker. Immediately following the swearing-in ceremony, the two of us headed in our vehicles to Regina, home to the RCMP training academy, otherwise known as Depot. We proved that being *far* too keen to get to Regina had its downside.

We arrived three days earlier than many of our troop mates. We were provided fatigues, our uniform, and assigned to a thirty-two-person dorm. The force's approach to policing being very paramilitary at the time, we soon learned that everyone we ran into was our superior. The status of raw recruits fell somewhere between rodents and trash.

My first full day could easily have been my last. We were assembled in the control room where we were introduced to Staff Sergeant Major W.D. Pomfret. We had just returned from having our heads shaved down to a brush cut. Pomfret's military style put the fear of God in me. He asked if anyone knew how to drive a vehicle. Having been told not to volunteer for anything, I stood with three other troop mates and said nothing. He then asked how the hell we got there, to which we all replied: by our cars. In response to this outburst (I was probably the loudest of the four), I was assigned to take his car and drive it to the wash bay, where we would make it shine. This order was followed by a stern warning not to put a mark on his police car.

I crossed the road from the guard shack and hopped in his vehicle, which was parked behind another police car. When I turned the key, the car started immediately and lunged into the back of the vehicle in front of it. "Damn it, who'd have thought it'd have a standard transmission!" I've never seen a man cross a road as quickly as Staff Sergeant Pomfret did then. I quickly received some military indoctrination. He told me that I was not worthy to breathe oxygen and that my time in Depot may be limited.

Following the worst berating of my early life, our drill instructor, Corporal Jim Schrumm, happened to be walking by. The staff sergeant major asked him if he had any room for such a rodent as myself, and that's how I was assigned to the RCMP Depot regimental band and to Schrumm's wrath for the next several months. Now, one must realize two things. First, I had never managed to master any musical instrument. And secondly, on May 23, not even three weeks away, Queen Elizabeth would be arriving to honour our one hundredth anniversary. There I was, a green rookie who didn't know how to march, who was unable to keep a beat to a hymn, and who was scared to death to make even the slightest mistake. The band would be leading the parade, and we were all expected to display precision drill (military-style marching) and orchestrate quality music.

Well, I did not disappoint. I successfully faked blowing the trumpet with the rest of the band members, marched into position, and came to attention standing in the back row of the band. It was a sweltering hot day and my first in the Red Serge (the red jacket of the RCMP's dress uniform). With my fear of screwing up I stood at attention looking like a statue. And then, just as we were about to step off, I completely passed out. I've been told that I stayed at attention and landed on the brim of my Stetson. My band members marched over me, and I ended up in the Depot hospital diagnosed with heat stroke. Strike two.

Our troop, Troop 4, was made up of a cross-section of men from across Canada ranging in age from nineteen to twenty-seven. We all possessed different backgrounds and all of us had different career aspirations. Training closely resembled military discipline; many of us learned to fear our drill instructors, who had a way of making even the strongest person feel less than human. While we could have done without their verbal abuse, the focus on discipline prepared us for dealing with difficult situations in the field, since nothing to follow could come close to what we experienced in Depot.

An event I can now look back on and laugh is a time when two of us were accused of looking at the infamous drill instructor Corporal Schrumm, resulting in his sending us to the chapel to kneel at the altar and pray out loud that "God would forgive us for we were dinks." Imagine a church full of tourists and two raw recruits, praying out loud with the corporal standing over them, yelling, "I can't hear you!" I am sure we made those tourists' day and likely for a few of them we became the subject of ridicule. I prided myself on having a strong sense of humour, so the more Schrumm bellowed that he could not hear us, the louder I got—somehow managing to keep a straight face!

We also received considerable training in self-defence, with a vast percentage of our time focused on ground-fighting. Although such military boot camp–style methods would likely not be considered admissible in today's environment, this training pitted one troop member against another for three-minute intervals. This enabled everyone to fully appreciate that the job of a police officer could result in unwanted confrontations so that in in the future, when faced with such a prospect, it would be ingrained in us that street fighting had no rules. To understand the differences between now and then, the only weapon provided then was a .38 revolver, whereas today there is a Glock revolver, baton, pepper spray and more often than not, a taser. Training today focuses on when to deploy which weapon based on our "wheel of force" training. We did not have these use-of-force options back then, so we learned that using our head to de-escalate a situation was the best option for everyone concerned, a fact I feel is sadly overlooked in today's training.

To illustrate this point, when I became chief of police of Cobourg, I attended Durham Regional Police's use-of-force training, which was a yearly requirement for all operational officers. During the exercise, a training officer in full protective gear simulates various aggressive scenarios. You are tested on whether you effectively deploy the correct weapon in each scenario. When the training officer came at me, having had VIP protection training, I quickly put him on the ground without having to use any of the use-of-force options. He called a timeout, indicating that I should have used a baton and that my actions were unacceptable. This is what is wrong with training today—you can club somebody with your baton, but if you use self-defence techniques, it's considered an error.

In my opinion, this is the reason we are seeing more and more officers being disciplined for excessive use of force. We need to go back to basics and let officers learn de-escalation skills prior to advancing the various use-of-force options.

Another unique rule was that everyone had to wear a fedora when we left the base. Although by today's standards this is an archaic ritual, it provided a day of bonding, as our troop members took great pride in choosing a hat regardless of how it looked. The fedora also had to be worn into the guardhouse after a free night out. On one occasion, several of my troop members and I arrived back at the guardhouse in my Volkswagen Beetle convertible. Most of my troop members were in no condition to walk into the guard-house and sign in. Seeing as I was the designated driver (which unfortunately did not mean I did not have a few drinks), I came to their rescue and put all my troop mates' hats on, one on top of the other. I marched in and signed a name, then took off a hat and signed another name. This was the one time my sense of humour saved the day. Corporal Schrumm said that since this was the first time anyone had tried this, he would let us get away with it without any penalty. I had missed another strike!

As I mentioned earlier, I had been volun-ordered to join the band. Even today, many members of the force feel that band members are slackers, since being in the band comes with several benefits, one of which is missing some morning parades. Although it wasn't something I would have done on my own, looking back I can say it provided phenomenal memories. Since it was our centennial year (1873–1973), we were invited to lead the Calgary Stampede and Regina's Buffalo Day parades. The Stampede permitted us time away from Depot and a free pass from Corporal Schrumm permitting us to attend a great party in Calgary. Many of us were suffering the next day as we led the parade, but it was well worth it.

Driver training was a sport for me—it included high-speed driving and pursuit driving, and driving techniques from the emergency-brake turn to the Y-turn. As I've mentioned, thanks to my brother Ron, I had driven many fast cars in all types of situations, so the first time my instructor told me to follow the other instructor and not lose him, they quickly learned I was not intimidated by speed or terrain. I successfully pursued the second instructor on country roads, fields, and eventually back to the main road. When I saw my personnel file years later, this same instructor wrote that he'd never before taught a driver with such a sense of humour regardless of the circumstances. As my father insisted, I learned to talk before walking, so I will gladly provide commentary during a pursuit.

Strike three came when I contracted mononucleosis in late September. I tried to fight through the sickness, but (short of death) it could not have been a worse case. I spent three weeks at the Regina General Hospital, putting me far behind my troop. In those days, the practice was to "back-squad" anyone who fell behind, which meant they'd be held back for additional training. I went into the hospital at 175 pounds and came out at 158. Upon my return I was the weakest member of my troop. I was summoned to the commanding officer's office, who said I likely would be put back three months. But I was determined, so I asked what I would need to do to graduate alongside my troop. The commanding officer told me I needed to complete all academics and pass my bronze medallion in swimming. I made a commitment to myself that I would pass all academics in the top 10 percent and would get my medallion.

Thanks to the support of my troop and all my instructors, I passed all the academics and came second in my troop. I barely achieved my swimming medallion, and I made it through the physical requirements largely due to my self-defence skills, but I guess sympathy won the day.

Finally, in November 1973, just a couple weeks prior to my twentieth birthday, graduation day arrived. That sense of accomplishment cannot be put into words. Training transformed many of us from teenagers into somewhat responsible young adults.

After graduation comes assignment. An interesting aspect of this era is that your assigned posting often takes interesting twists. At this time hockey was prominently played in many of the divisions. (Most provinces have a single RCMP division, usually designated by a letter, e.g., Ontario is O Division, Quebec is C, Alberta is K, British Columbia is E, and Saskatchewan is F, while Regina is Depot. Ottawa has two divisions: HQ for Headquarters and National, formerly A.)[3] My posting had more to do with the fact that the Chilliwack sub-division needed a goalie than with my own personal preference. Thus I was relocated to Langley, British

CHAPTER TWO

Columbia, and so began a career that enabled me to work on serial murders, break bread with some of Canada's most notable criminals, and travel around the world—which at times meant experiencing coca and poppy eradications in Colombia on a gunship helicopter. I spent the first few months living in Richmond with my cousin and her husband, who was a Vancouver PD officer, which helped immensely with the homesickness.

Chapter Three

LANGLEY DETACHMENT

When I left Regina for Langley, I was so naïve, I thought to get to Vancouver, you just went up one side of a mountain and came down the other, lickety-split. The drive to Langley was incredible—I was dumbfounded both by the scenic beauty and the long distance. During my drive I stopped overnight in Revelstoke and decided to check in to the local RCMP detachment. (A "detachment" is a section of the RCMP that polices its local area.) Although I do not recall the member's name, we went on patrol together and he took me to fingerprint an individual who had been tragically killed going over a cliff in his eighteen-wheeler. Nothing can prepare a person for such a gruesome scene. At nineteen, seeing a body in such a decimated state shocked me into the reality of what the life of a police officer can be.

The rest of my journey was uneventful. I arrived in Langley and reported to the detachment. When I entered the office of Staff Sergeant George Allen, the detachment's commander, I came to attention and called him "sir." I quickly learned that Langley was not like Depot back in Regina: here, only commissioned officers were to be called "sir." He told me that hockey would be starting soon and I would be expected to play for Chilliwack but would also be expected to make up all shifts.

I'll be mentioning the various ranks of members of the RCMP throughout the book. For those who are unfamiliar with the ranking system, let me take a moment to list them, in order of highest rank to lowest, with commissioned officers ranking above non-commissioned officers.

Commissioned officers:
- commissioner
- deputy commissioner
- associate deputy minister
- senior assistant deputy minister
- assistant commissioner
- chief superintendent
- superintendent
- inspector

Non-commissioned officers:
- sergeant major
- staff sergeant major
- staff sergeant
- sergeant
- corporal
- constable

Now that I had graduated, I was a newly minted constable. Langley could not have been a better training ground. I was the nineteenth member on strength and soon learned we were one of the busiest detachments in the lower mainland, thereby requiring new recruits to become self-reliant almost immediately. As a young officer, I was exposed to all levels of crime. My trainer was Ken Sarnecki. Shortly after meeting him I explained I wanted to be attached to a drug section. Ken, who had about seven years' service, laughed and explained I should not even consider it for at least eight years. Clearly Ken did not know me. Eight years was not in the cards. I quickly ingratiated myself with the Langley detachment's General Investigative Section (GIS) and in particular the corporal in charge, Les Bannerman. I worked my uniform shift and then volunteered to work with GIS, hoping to pick up as many investigative skills from seasoned members (such as Ron Hurt and Norm Leibel, whom I still hold in high regard) as I could.

I seemed to have a knack for enlisting cooperative individuals who eagerly provided me information on the local drug scene. I gained a reputation as a focused investigator with a bent toward drug enforcement. My fearless appearance (which contrasted with my inner reality) resulted in the GIS unit calling on me on many occasions to assist them. They were mainly minor tasks, but I was called on nevertheless.

One event that still haunts me today involved three murders of young women over a short period of time. All the murders had the same pattern. Although I played only a minor investigative role, the death of these women made me realize just how precious life is and how quickly it can be taken by the worst of individuals. I also realized that police work requires high-level skills and a keen mind willing and able to examine the most innocuous of details. Sadly, these crimes were not solved. To the best of my knowledge, they remain cold cases today.

Some of my early experiences involved attending accident scenes, many of which are still vivid in my mind. These events are of such significance for the Langley detachment, they've practically gained mythic status, becoming part of the detachment's lore. The first occurred shortly after my arrival and was one of the first times I was on patrol by myself. I got called to an accident in Fort Langley where, allegedly, a vehicle had overturned on the train tracks. Upon my arrival in the early-morning hours, I found an overturned pickup with a lone male whose arm was pinned between the roof of the car and the train tracks. The freight train was due. According to the radio operator, I was *somewhat* loud when I called in about the need to radio the train—despite yelling into the mic, communicating to the office *through my radio*—and after that, I became known as the constable who *really* did *not* need a radio.

I was told the train may not be able to stop in time. The man, who had been drinking, asked me to hack his arm off in lieu of being hit by the train. I went as far as getting the axe from the cruiser and agreeing that if the train could not be stopped, I would get him out one way or the other. Fortunately, I never had to test whether or not I could have gone through with taking his arm off. The train did stop. But the light of the train was too close for comfort.

The second accident involved a lone male who'd missed a curve in an MG, resulting in it flipping on top of him. I noted the male as *pinned under the car.* When the ambulance arrived, the attendant, Tony, checked his vitals, something I had already done. Because of the car's pressure on his chest, we could not get a pulse, and I had not seen any sign of breathing. I opined that there was not much that could be done for him. Because of the hopelessness of the situation, we did not rush to get the car off him; we were taking photographs of a scene we believed to be a fatality. When the tow truck showed up and began removing the vehicle, he crawled out, still inebriated, and berated us for taking so long. I had known Tony for several months, but I can't remember him ever before turning as white as he did that night, like he had seen a ghost.

In August 1975 I was called to an accident in Aldergrove where a young girl had been struck by a car. The girl was bleeding from the mouth, not breathing. I cleared her airway as best I could and gave mouth-to-mouth. She began breathing. The corporal in charge of traffic, Kent Hansen, arrived and saw blood all over my face; I explained the circumstances. The young girl's survival is a positive outcome that this police officer looks back on with pride. Kent recommended me for a Meritorious Award, which I proudly received, but the fact the girl survived was truly the only recognition I sought.

On another occasion working with Kent, we attended an accident on Fraser Highway in which a young lady was struck turning into her parents' driveway. I was assigned traffic control, as this was a busy two-lane highway with one lane totally blocked by the crash. Her father kept trying to cross the road to get to her vehicle. We had to warn him several times to wait until I finished moving traffic. The moment I turned back to the traffic, directing cars through, I heard a thud and saw the father rolling off the hood of a vehicle. Even though we'd asked him several times to wait until directed, the fact that he was struck really affected me. I blamed myself for not recognizing the shock he must have been in. Luckily traffic was not moving quickly and his injuries were minor in nature. His daughter lived.

One other event that haunts me to this day involved a single-car accident and the death of a young man. It was Sunday morning, and his sister and brother-in-law had come to the detachment in Langley to report their brother missing, as he was supposed to have been on his way home Saturday evening. I cannot explain it, but I got a premonition—I saw the vehicle upside down in a water-filled ditch on River Road. I remember saying to Sergeant Ken Robinson, "I will do a patrol. I think I know where the car is." Sure enough, I drove to the exact spot and found the vehicle just as I had envisioned: in a water-filled ditch, upside down. I am not sure how to explain this, but something like this happened once before when my parents were in an accident in Elmira. It was a bad accident at an intersection; both lived with minor injuries. I am not sure why these premonitions happened. They have not occurred since.

In June of 1975 I had one of my only police-car accidents, which was due to stupidity, or maybe carelessness (my own), more than anything else. I was visiting my then girlfriend (now wife), Lee, at her parents' place, sitting in the driveway, when a call came—an officer needing backup. I let my ego assume control and I immediately put on my lights and siren. I backed down my future in-laws' long gravel laneway, which had trees lining either side. Somewhere around halfway I lost control of the car and ping-ponged off the trees, damaging both them and the cruiser extensively. Embarrassed, scolded by Lee, I called my corporal, who broke out laughing at my stupidity when he arrived on the scene. My report stated that I lost control because I was overzealous "due to my concern for a colleague." I was found guilty of a minor degree of negligence, a lenient charge. Had I been found guilty of full negligence, I would have had to pay some of the costs of the damage.

I learned valuable lessons while being introduced to the world of bikers (and one serial killer who'd managed to elude justice for forty years): how to manage informants and ensure their anonymity; how to hone interview skills, which I believe I was able to master through my work as an undercover operator; how to relate to anyone and at any level of a criminal organization. And yet, through all the important cases I worked while at Langley, it would be disingenuous not to talk about the stupid stunts we officers pulled on each other.

One night, we dressed a mannequin in jeans and an old shirt and "hanged" it in a cell, as we had an arrestee who was on suicide watch. That individual had been moved to the women's cells and thus was—intentionally, on our part—not in the line of sight of what we were doing. We called the corporal and communicated that there had been an incident in the cells. As he walked down the cell hall, he could see a shadow of what appeared to be a person hanging. I will not repeat the language that flowed at this point, and it was not until he got to the cell block that he apprehended the reality of our prank. What we did not factor in was how this stunt may have affected our corporal, who had years of service and likely had seen a few suicides in his career. We got the reaction we'd expected but, immature as we were, failed to consider the potential emotional consequences of our jest.

A few other stunts we pulled off: Having a new member go to the morgue at Langley Memorial Hospital, open a drawer, and yelp in terror when his supervisor sat up. Convincing a new member to shine a spotlight into the night sky from the field next to the detachment, him believing he was helping the RCMP land a helicopter. Perhaps the most asinine stunt I witnessed was when two members came to the home of myself and two other members, affectionately known as Glover Road Detachment. My housemates were my partner Larry Campbell and Brian Leight. We'd been sleeping soundly until the two officers came into my room and fired three shots into my mattress. To this day I scratch my head at this. The experience certainly did nothing to alleviate what was later diagnosed as PTSD.

Two other RCMP members lived with me at "Glover Road Detachment": Al Jensen and Brian Millette. Later, another housemate, Bob Outhwaite, joined Glover Road. During my uniform days, Al and I had a standing bet—if we were both working and were in opposite ends of our jurisdiction when an alarm went off in Langley City, the last person to arrive at the alarm location had to buy the beer. As you might imagine, this resulted in some turbo-speed light-and-siren responses. On one occasion when the alarm was in the heart of Langley, I raced to the city and at a T-intersection turned a fast right. I had forgotten there'd been an accident about four years earlier; a car had gone straight through the intersection. This was in front of Ward and Tout Jewelers, where my future mother-in-law worked. As it happened, she was looking out the window and clearly saw how close I came to parking the vehicle in the store. To make matters worse, when I got to the bank, I jumped out of the car with the police lights still on and locked the door, leaving my keys in the car. Officially, I won, and I got my beers, but this was the end of our agreement.

Despite some of our irresponsible antics (which serve to evidence that most men's brains do not fully mature until their late twenties), I was able to rack up many drug arrests thanks to the collaborative work of a significant number of informants. Starting in December 1975, my detachment's commander allowed me to work drugs full time, which for more senior members was not welcoming news. While the lack of support from certain members could have been discouraging, I was buoyed by the help of the GIS, uniform members, and my phenomenal informants. Together we made some impressive drug arrests. In one such event I had received a call just before Christmas from an unknown male, stating *2400 Avenue, under the hay.* No more, no less. Armed with this information, we conducted surveillance, resulting in one of the largest drug seizures in the area at that time, including bales of marijuana, cocaine, heroin, and methamphetamine. To this day we do not know the source of the information.

Part Two

THE BEGINNING OF UNDERCOVER

Chapter Four

THE LAUNCH OF MY UNDERCOVER PERSONA

In 1975, my desire to expand my knowledge in drug enforcement paid off; I was recruited into undercover training. We received three weeks of intensive training in Montreal from skilled officers who had infiltrated criminal groups. The lead instructor was Doug Ewing, recognized for his abilities to do just that.

The training awoke my desire to focus on organized-crime groups, as I realized it was only through combatting the highest levels that society could ever gain ground against criminal activity. Also, after reading a number of stories undertaken by investigative journalists, I understood that a good scam with a believable story could cause nearly anyone or any organization to be infiltrated. My confidence in my ability to do so scared the hell out of many of my peers and bosses—we took a lot of risks, consistently pushing the envelope, believing these were all calculated risks.

Montreal, a diverse city known to have lots of street drugs, mainly marijuana, hashish, and cocaine, was the best city in which to hone undercover skills at that time. One exercise we undertook provided an opportunity to meet with an individual who had been injured by an explosive device, allegedly during an FLQ operation. This kind of exposure to society's underbelly provided us with the confidence needed for concocting stories plausible enough to gain us access to criminal groups.

During our three weeks of training, we made a multitude of minor purchases of marijuana and hashish in the amounts decided on by the training team. This was done to demonstrate an operator's ability to function in various settings under differing controls. At this time cocaine was virtually impossible to come across—everyone agreed it had been cut so many times it wasn't worth purchasing. During one of the exercises, my colleague and I were able to negotiate a three- to five-pound hashish transaction, which was significant during this era. But seeing as this was a training exercise, we were not allowed to go through with a purchase of this volume.

To test our ability to adapt and think on our feet, we were sent into a gay bar and told that we had to be able to fit in. I was still a young member and, for the most part, relatively naïve, so this was a tremendously challenging development exercise, as it forced those of us who participated to dig deep into our acting skills. Following the undercover training, I returned to the Langley detachment and was sent back into uniform by the staff sergeant despite the fact that I had long hair and needed to keep it that way for the purposes of a soon-to-be-assigned undercover project. My appearance resulted in a cartoon hitting the front page of the local paper and subsequent directions from Headquarters to get me out of uniform. Thanks to the power of the press, I was transferred back to the drug section. Like many young officers, I had gained the newfound belief that I was infallible and capable of infiltrating any criminal element.

Maybe our attitudes didn't help the situation, but I came to realize that the young undercover (U/C) officers were often viewed with disdain by senior commissioned officers, who saw many of us as a necessary evil. They felt our long hair and beards had no place in the force. One morning I got on the elevator at the RCMP's

Vancouver headquarters with two uniformed senior officers. I, along with two drug investigative colleagues, had long hair, jeans, and a T-shirt on. One of the senior officers told the other that what he was seeing was the reason the force was such a mess today. At this juncture in my career, I realized that there is a substantial difference in the skill sets necessary to carrying out federal enforcement versus contract policing. Federal policing requires proactivity and defined investigative skills, whereas contract policing is, for the most part, reactive.

I suspect that much of society believes that undercover work is exactly like what you see in the movies: glamour, fast cars, and luxury hotels. Retired staff sergeant Hugh Stewart summed up the reality in the pages of my 1981 annual assessment:

> An undercover operation can best be described as stress filled, at worst. The strain on team members, both mental and physical, defies description. An undercover operator must first and foremost be a good investigator. With this as a foundation he/she then must be able to mould body and mind to fit the character of the criminal he/she portrays, throughout remembering he/she is a police officer. Difficult, to say the least.

To be effective undercover, you need to have an excellent memory to describe, in as much detail as possible, the events surrounding the initial meeting and any subsequent dealings with a target. In practice, this often meant that following a late night of work, it would be necessary to spend hours detailing the activities, sometimes into the early-morning hours. It was not unusual to spend four to five hours writing notes.

We need to differentiate between the skills of federal officers and the skills of contract officers. This reality has become magnified throughout my career, leading me to the conclusion that the RCMP needs to focus primarily on its federal responsibilities and enable provinces and municipalities to manage its contract-policing requirements. This view has only solidified through the years. The best analogy I can give is this: Would you want a heart specialist performing your brain surgery? Throughout my career I have often expressed my belief that organized crime and transnational criminal activity are complex and mandate the need for highly skilled investigators. These skills take time to germinate. There must, therefore, be an official recognition that federal policing, whether it be RCMP or another stand-alone organization, demands specialized skills if Canada wants to be seen as an effective partner on the world stage. In the time since I've started writing this book, the RCMP has started recruiting members with specialized skills, e.g., accounting, law, and computer science (to thwart cybercrime). A specialized training program has also been created which does not require members to go to Regina.

During this period, I learned a valuable lesson that could have resulted in my being seriously injured. Information had been received that a group of people were actively dealing in large amounts of marijuana. I did a cold call with two uniform members present. A cold call is when you call a target on the phone out of the blue, and it requires coming up with a viable story as to how you acquired the phone number. Whatever we said must have been believable—I convinced the target to meet with me to complete a transaction involving marijuana. A fact that I should have taken into consideration: I had worked in Langley for two years by this point and had become known in the drug scene as the local narc.

The first meeting went well, and I was able to convince the contact I was a legitimate buyer. After I was introduced to a second person, the next step was for me to travel to an apartment complex to meet the supplier. Common sense should have told me that I would eventually run across someone who knew me, but I let my ego get the best of me and accompanied the two individuals to the apartment. They knocked on the door, and when the resident answered, he immediately asked his two colleagues why they'd brought a narc to his door. They jumped me, and I was beaten for a few minutes before my saviour Constable Ginny Zalis arrived and jumped on one of their backs, which enabled me to get my arms free. Constable Bob Outhwaite arrived shortly after, and we were able to gain control. The scariest moment was listening to them talk about getting me into the apartment so they could "do me."

I ended up in the hospital. Though I had suffered somewhat of a beating, the worst bruising was that of my ego. It was a hard lesson, but one that made me realize the danger that exists when working undercover. After this, I adopted the strategy of only taking measured risks—though that still didn't stop me from operating with a certain amount of bravado.

On another occasion, our General Investigative Section was investigating a series of break and enters. I had received confidential information about the culprits' identities, so a few members of the team opted to go and talk to them at the two-room shack where they resided. As my team members were speaking with the alleged culprits, I crawled up into the attic of the shack. Shortly after my colleagues left, the two suspects came inside and started talking about how happy they were that we had not found the drugs and the stolen property. I was writing notes up there like crazy. Somewhere in this conversation they started talking about how they'd like to get me alone so they could straighten me out, seeing how I seemed to always be involved in arrests. For some strange and bombastic reason, I swung down out of the attic and said, "Merry Christmas, and you are going to jail." The fight was on. Both suspects were arrested shortly after my colleagues entered the fray. This was prior to the Charter—at that time evidence was evidence, regardless of circumstances, unless the administration of justice was brought into disrepute. (You might ask what would cause justice to be brought into disrepute; that might look like a suspect's rights not being respected by officers, or an investigation being conducted in an unprofessional manner.) Looking back, I find my actions anything but professional, though in that era, arguably, they worked.

Langley was also where I met Lee, a woman who has stood by my side through unbelievable times, including three alleged contracts (one which I mentioned earlier; I'll discuss the others in more detail later in this book). I could not have found a more supportive life partner. Throughout my career, until my retirement, she put up with my work-comes-first ethic, which involved phone calls at all hours of the night, irregular work schedules, and long hours away from home, and sometimes far too much drinking. She has been the one constant in my life. And, never one to involve herself in the politics of the RCMP, she's kept me grounded all these years.

Chapter Five

TORONTO UNDERCOVER ASSIGNMENT

In late 1975, I was selected to travel to Toronto where I would be engaged in a multijurisdictional undercover operation. The morning I left, I asked Lee to marry me. It was not under the best circumstances—we got engaged as she was leaving for work and I was heading out the door to the airport, not a very romantic engagement—but I would have crossed an ocean to get Lee to marry me. At the time, Lee was the Cloverdale Rodeo queen and showed horses, so I accepted that I wasn't only getting a wife, but also entry into the world of horse ownership.

During this assignment I met Kenneth Ingram "Kim" Marsh, another operator assigned to Vancouver Drugs. Residing under the same roof for six months, we became lifelong professional friends and teammates on many other assignments throughout our careers.

When we arrived in Toronto we initially stayed at the Sheraton, which had a great disco bar at that time. That week, we met our team and were briefed on the expectations for the operation, which we anticipated lasting six months or longer.

THE TEAM

The project plan called for the Toronto Police Service, the Ontario Provincial Police, and the RCMP to form a task force and work together to tackle the drug situation in Toronto. Some notable members involved included:

Inspector Seth Guinther. Seth was the drug enforcement branch's reporting officer for the Ontario region of the RCMP and was therefore responsible for reviewing reports and receiving financial approvals. He was gentle in his approach and extremely easy to relate to. He also came to support me following a misstep at a trial that could have gone very badly.

Sergeant Wayne Horrocks, a.k.a. Mr. Twiggy. Wayne was an East Coaster and a large, powerful man with a tremendous sense of humour. He served as the overall supervisor for the day-to-day operations, ensuring investigations progressed in a professional manner and that reports were submitted on time. Wayne loved his big cigars and was often seen with one hanging from his mouth during meetings. His cigar habit and his size actually worked against us at one point—our accused received a mild sentence, as the court ruled that he was likely intimidated by Wayne. Additionally, Wayne was a strong supporter of Patrick Kelly, likely causing him to gloss over what should have been red flags, which would soon become evident to everyone.

Corporal Ken St. Germain, a.k.a. "the Animal." Ken looked like he had gone several rounds with Muhammad Ali. He could play the part of an organized-crime street enforcer without much acting. He was what I would define as one of the casualties of having been exposed to the drug world for far too long a period, which stalled any opportunity for career progression. His isolation in his later years may have contributed to his early death. Ken was instrumental in playing my boss whenever a wannabe biker pulled a gun during a buy.

Constable Paul Byers. Paul was assigned from the Toronto Police Service and had worked with a famous homicide-and-robbery squad. He was what I would refer to as one tough street cop and was nicknamed "Pigpen." Through Paul, I was treated to numerous stories about the former Toronto detectives Lou Nicolucci and Frank Barbetta; that information proved invaluable in a later assignment in Vancouver and resulted in my acceptance into organized crime.

Mike Hayes, a.k.a. "Isaac." Mike was the other undercover operator assigned to this combined force team from the OPP. Mike was older and had been around longer than Kim and me, and in my view he was one of the funniest jokers I met in my career. I think he missed his calling as a stand-up comedian. We were always entertained whenever Mike was around. Once we were pulled over by uniform law enforcement and he surprised us all when he showed his badge, as it was not protocol for undercover officers to carry our badges on us.

Constable Patrick Kelly, a.k.a. "Irish." At the time, Pat was considered an outstanding undercover operator, a rising star in the force. Pat was assigned to work with me. A lot of what occurred when we worked together is explained by what was later uncovered about Pat. More on this later.

Reality set in when we were provided our undercover safehouse accommodations. Although we had a penthouse suite near the 401 and the Don Valley Parkway, the furniture consisted of barrack beds and low-rent furniture. This was not the vision we had been told to imagine during our undercover training. Toronto in the mid-seventies was not the Toronto we see today. I found the city to be like any other former industrial city, the older buildings all covered in soot. Going to a bar meant putting up with people smoking everywhere, and the seedier bars were subject to many fights, requiring a doorman to keep the peace.

The Toronto Police Service had bright yellow police cars that were visible from miles away. The street corners had roasted-chestnut vendors and Yonge Street was referred to as the "Sin Strip."[4] This was where all the action was, from Bloor to King, and many of the bars, drug dealers, and prostitutes were in this area.

The El Mocambo on Spadina was a venue of choice and continually brought in some acclaimed bands and artists. One evening, I heard the legendary violinist Papa John Creach play. The El Mocambo provided a place to be seen and absorb the culture. To "fit in," so to speak.

Our undercover operator team consisted of Mike Hayes, Kim Marsh, and me. We were immediately put to work, meeting with individuals identified by police drug teams throughout Toronto. The intelligence supported the belief that these targets were all actively dealing in various illicit drugs. Only eight days into the operation, I was involved in my first-ever purchase: a bundle of heroin being sold in Toronto's Little Italy. This was also my first lesson in being "ripped," since the "heroin" turned out not to be heroin at all. As soon as I realized, I had to take immediate action: contact the supplier and demand my money back.

When we finally connected, the suppliers gave me the third degree. They were surprised that I had not contacted them immediately after the sale, since they'd also found out that what was being provided to them for resale was only icing sugar. I explained that being new in town and not knowing the area well had delayed my reaching out. In order to maintain credibility in a tight spot like this, it is imperative to feign total displeasure, to come as close to the line of criminal threat of bodily harm for being ripped as you can, otherwise you'll be seen as a narc.

Many street-level traffickers are also users and will do anything to avoid having to make up for any losses—given that chasing their next fix tends to be their primary goal, these dealers aren't the type to honour a deal and pay back a loss. Over a period of almost two weeks, I held meeting after meeting with various individuals in the Italian district, all introduced to me at the time I'd purchased the initial bundle. But the supplier became avoidant, and that operation failed.

From this point on we needed to dig deep within ourselves to use our skills to try to meet identified drug suppliers either in person or over the phone, after having landed on a viable story as to how we'd come across the individual's number or go-to drinking establishment. My story—about being from Vancouver and not knowing a lot of people in Toronto—taught me the need for patience and perseverance, as it did nothing to entrench credibility with our drug targets. Each time, they'd grill me about who I knew and how I'd come across their name. Working closely with Pat Kelly, a man I then knew only as a seasoned operator, enabled me to pick up some great lines. I learned to never provide any verifiable alibi since "Simpsons doesn't tell Eaton's its business."

We were briefed on who was involved in organized crime, from Johnny "Pops" Papalia, to Paul Volpe, to the Musitano Brothers, to Cosimo Commisso. It was well known at the outset that the organized-crime groups were high-value targets and difficult to infiltrate. As a result, we focused on entrepreneurial groups (most of whom had indirect links to organized crime) and individuals.

As the Toronto assignment unfolded, I honed my undercover skills and worked on my undercover persona—which could involve anything from researching backstory and connections, to memorizing personal facts, to deciding on catchphrases and language register, to practising being "in persona" with other officers, to shopping for my persona's clothes and accessories. At this time, Pat Kelly was deemed to be one of the best undercover operators the RCMP had.

Given our mutual interest in Canadiana-style antiques, I hit it off with him and therefore ended up working on numerous cases with him. During this era, a cover team was only provided when we were in the process of carrying out a buy, otherwise we were left to our own devices to frequent nightclubs and afterhours clubs.

Kim and I spent many weekends visiting clubs like the El Mocambo and other afterhours clubs that existed at the time. Looking back, I am not sure this was a good use of our time; however, it was what was asked of us, so we wholeheartedly agreed. The many hours we spent in these clubs, although ingratiating ourselves with the local scene, did not result in a lot of drug purchases. Any that occurred were low-level street purchases. This type of purchase was essentially useless and did nothing to slow down the drug trade or identify the major criminals behind the flow of street drugs.

My team had been tasked with meeting individuals engaged in trafficking cocaine, heroin, speed, hashish, and marijuana. This operation essentially ran without the use of informants; therefore, we were required to meet with the potential targets ourselves. Mike Hayes (the joker, and a seasoned officer) was very successful in this because he looked the part of the grizzled fringe biker and could engage with a more defined criminal element, including the bikers.

In order to work in the drug milieu, it was necessary to learn techniques simulating the use of certain illegal drugs. Without exposing any trade secrets, I was able to simulate injecting heroin, smoking pot, and snorting cocaine, all of which had to be witnessed by the other users—and believed. But I wasn't taught how to simulate drinking hash tea. On one occasion prior to a buy, the supplier brewed hash tea and handed me a cup. This is where you learn to think on your feet. As I turned to walk to the seating area, I feigned that I'd tripped and spilled the tea. Fortunately, the supplier wanted to punish me, so he told me I would not be offered another cup. It is great when a plan comes together.

I was able to make purchases from a range of dealers: from street-level dealers to mid-level dealers of coke, heroin, and methamphetamine, most of whom were users. Some days, I ran into individuals who resided in the richest parts of Toronto (e.g., Forest Hill), living in what would be multimillion-dollar homes today. Other days, I encountered people who lived in rooming houses, scraping by, focused on how to get their daily fix. This operation made me realize that no one is immune to drug addiction. This is a fact we are witnessing today with the fentanyl crisis. Vancouver's safe-supply program has made middle- to upper-income addictions more prevalent. Recent studies have shown that the safe-supply program is failing our citizens on several fronts. The drugs being provided to addicts are not strong enough to meet their needs and therefore some of these issued drugs are being diverted, which is allegedly resulting in more youth using these and becoming addicted. The fentanyl on the street is so strong, and so addictive, that many professionals are also getting hooked. Addictions are a health problem that should not be dealt with through arrests and incarceration. Some of the arrests we made were young upper-class adults and youth who'd gotten hooked and started selling to maintain their addiction. It made me realize that the young women who prostituted themselves often did so primarily for their daily fix and sometimes under the control of a pimp who was also a drug user or dealer. Drugs do not discriminate. Regardless of profession or stature in society, any life can become dictated by a drug addiction. Unfortunately, at this time in the seventies, society demanded criminal charges even for the smallest amount of drugs and did not differentiate marijuana from heroin, as both were equally illegal under the Narcotic Control Act.

After ten months the operation wound down. The U/C team's combined efforts contributed to eighty-four persons being charged, and 143

charges related to trafficking in cocaine, methamphetamine, heroin, and morphine. There was
an indication that some of the accused wanted
to exact revenge on us and that a veiled threat
had been made. Kim and I were returning to our
posts in British Columbia; for us, the danger only
existed during our trial commitments in Toronto.
The RCMP undercover program coordinator
obtained our treasury board's approval for us to
fly first class, which meant we could board last and
disembark first. Kim and I were in our early twenties, so flying first class in the 747 with bar service
was an experience of a lifetime. Our reasoning was
also that the free drinks would ensure, should we be
attacked, that we would not feel any pain. I should
mention: with Kim and I were travelling together,
both of us in blue jeans and with longer hair—we
really did not look like we belonged in first class.
Two businessmen started grilling us about why we
were in first class. Not missing a beat, we told him
our "old man" was rich and we were just enjoying
his money. I think this ruined the trip for these
two well-dressed gentlemen, but it stopped them
from asking any more questions.

Lee and I married in the fall of 1976. We honeymooned in
Ontario, since I had to testify in a court case flowing from the
undercover assignment. I had previously testified at the preliminary
hearing pertaining to a cocaine purchase off a guy by the name of
Jimmy Pitaro, the owner of Colis Camera Shop in Toronto. The
introduction to Pitaro involved an informant who had worked with
the force at very high levels for a number of years. I'd been given
explicit directions not to reveal that an informant was involved. The

day of the preliminary hearing, I was asked about "the individual who introduced [me] to Pitaro" and to explain his role. I told them I did not know who they were speaking of. I thought that was the end of it.

I will say, I owe Jimmy Pitaro's lawyer, Mr. Eddie Greenspan, my career. On the first day of Pitaro's trial, I admitted to misleading the court during the preliminary hearing to protect an informant. There were two reasons I had tried to hide the informant's involvement. For one, I'd been instructed by my superiors not to reveal his name, and secondly, there had been another buy, facilitated by my informant, from the son of a former Toronto officer who had been killed in the line of duty. On the advice of management, charges were not laid in that case, a decision that was taken almost immediately following my transaction with the fallen officer's son. Mr. Greenspan was given leeway by the court to pursue a line of questioning regarding my revelation, but instead he chose to accept my circumstances as self-explanatory and asked no further questions.

Pitaro's arrest was interesting in and of itself. I had attended Pitaro's residence with Paul Byers and made the arrest with him, a fact that would never happen today, as the U/C operators no longer get involved in arrests. It was in the heart of Little Italy, and several neighbours congregated near our unmarked car. Pitaro's mother tried to lie in front of the car so we couldn't leave. Once we got Pitaro to the RCMP booking area, he was interviewed by Wayne Horrocks, dangling cigar and all. And that was when, due to Wayne's size and penchant for stogies, the jury requested the judge give him leniency. As I mentioned, Pitaro got it.

I honestly believed my career was over the day I testified and revealed the falsehood in my preliminary testimony. Judge Hogue, who I had appeared before many times in other criminal cases, admonished me. He warned me that he'd be following up with my superiors. I felt terrible and was concerned about a potential perjury charge. But the fact that I'd come forward myself with the info and had only been trying to distance myself from a well-placed informant resulted in a recommendation that no further action be taken. Inspector Seth Guinther was briefed on what transpired. He was very supportive. Thereafter I promised myself I'd be absolutely straightforward in any future testimony I provided.

PAT KELLY AS PARTNER

With Pat Kelly's assistance as my boss, I infiltrated a plethora of mid-level heroin, cocaine, speed, and hashish trafficking networks. And if you were wondering earlier, this Pat Kelly is one and the same as the ex-RCMP convicted for murdering his wife, Jeannette Kelly. Michael Harris's book *The Judas Kiss: The Undercover Life of Patrick Kelly* painted the true picture of Pat—that he was a sociopath who believed he was smarter than the system in which he served. As I look back on the operation, I think of the TV show *NCIS* and the character Leroy Jethro Gibbs (played by Mark Harmon), who says, "Rule #39: There is no such thing as a coincidence."

As I think back on purchases I made with Pat, I realize that it's likely some of them were totally orchestrated by Pat and that the "buy" money may never have been paid. One buy in particular involved a quarter pound of heroin from a group we referred to as "the Jewish connection." I vividly remember arguing with the team that the demanded price of three thousand dollars per ounce would not be paid, seeing as ounces cost less than half this much in Vancouver. Unfortunately, Pat won the day. He alleged that this was the price he'd negotiated. When we did the take-down, the two accused admitted to supplying the heroin, but they denied ever receiving any money. Of course, at the time this was dismissed outright as a lie, but as Pat's life unravelled, I can see it is likely no money ever changed hands.

There were a tremendous number of red flags that should have caused management to delve into Kelly's file, to pay closer attention to his behaviour. Prior to that undercover assignment, Kelly had allegedly been working in an undercover capacity for Jim Alford. There was supposed to be a "flash roll," which is when money, often a bundle of banknotes rolled up with an elastic, is shown to get drugs and then immediate arrests are made. When Kelly gave the signal for investigators to make the arrest, the flash-roll money could not be located, despite extensive searching. Alford mused that the only way the money could have disappeared is that it was never taken by the target into their location. Since Kelly "walked on water" in the eyes of the Ontario RCMP management, his contention that money was left at the location was taken at face value. I now believe that some of the purchases made with Kelly were arranged by him so that he could pocket the buy money. While I cannot prove it, there is a strong possibility that's what was happening.

Where there is smoke there is often fire. Allegations cannot be dismissed without an independent investigation. The Kelly story stoked my desire to fight corruption for the remainder of my career. Anyone, and I mean anyone, can be co-opted under the right set of circumstances, a fact I witnessed throughout my time with the RCMP. (By "co-opt," I mean to have someone agree to do something for you that may not be on the up and up. Once the initial action has been taken, the person co-opted becomes bound to the co-opting party. This can be done through bribes or blackmail.) But it wasn't until Hong Kong that I was able to see the value of having an independent body mandated to investigate corruption prior to an allegation being dismissed.

When the operation ended, I moved out of the safehouse and moved in with Pat and Jeannette. Kelly claimed he was making inordinate amounts of money selling antiques. He had definitely studied Canadiana-style antiques and was able to obtain items for a very select clientele. He bragged about making money hand over fist selling mounted polar-bear rugs. This was his explanation for the fact that we went out to dinner most nights and ate like royalty.

What I know for sure is that the daily stipend for food was not close to offsetting our fancy meals.

My wife and I stayed with Pat and Jeannette Kelly on two occasions at their hundred-year-old renovated farmhouse in Cookstown. Our first visit was following the quarter-pound heroin seizure from "the Jewish connection" and the second was when Lee and I stayed over for a few days during our honeymoon. Cookstown is a quaint village in Simcoe County about an hour and a half north of Toronto. The old farmhouse had a new addition—a floor-to-ceiling stone fireplace. Pat and Jeannette appeared to be a happily married couple who enjoyed travel. Their house in Cookstown was what Lee and I considered a dream home, one that was definitely out of our price range and our ability to acquire as a young police family. We left believing Pat and Jeannette had a tremendous life ahead of them.

I learned the truth about the real Pat Kelly much later. Pat joined the force in 1970, three years before I did, and through what appeared to be a true aptitude for undercover, the RCMP sent him to the Javeriana University in Bogotá, Colombia, to receive total Spanish immersion. Jeannette, an airline hostess with Avianca, met Pat in Bogotá, leading to their romance and marriage. In 1978, the Cookstown home was destroyed by fire. Kelly claimed this was a result of his U/C activities. Although it was strongly believed even at the time that Kelly set the fire, the initial arson charges were dismissed and the insurance paid out.

Following the fire, Jeannette and Pat were no longer getting along. He was supposedly having numerous affairs, including the wife of a force member who had separated from her husband and had moved in with them. On March 29, 1981, Jeannette fell to her death at the apartment in Toronto she and Pat Kelly shared. Although the life insurance paid out the death benefits, Kelly was later charged and convicted of murder.

As the murder investigation unfolded, it came to light that Kelly worked for wealthy Colombians who wanted to get their money into Europe or the United States, a hustle that had allegedly been set up during his time language training in Colombia.

Initially, like many other members who worked with Kelly, we found this unfathomable. I kept reflecting back, however, on what Jim Alford had said about the missing money. Reality set in. Initially, there was a feeling of betrayal, and later some embarrassment— we're supposed to be able to detect suspicious activity! It's no wonder that investigative teams can lose sight of objectivity leading to false arrests. But from this day forward, I operated with the view that I would rather take down a dirty cop than an organized-crime figure.

Returning to Langley, I initially went back into uniform, but this was short-lived, and I found myself back in the drug section. Over the course of the next couple of years I travelled about thirty-five times between Vancouver and Toronto to testify in court. We continued to make our mark on the drug community, resulting in several more well-known criminals being arrested and incarcerated.

Chapter Six

TEN THOUSAND DOLLARS
FOR A LIFE

During one of my trips back to Toronto for court, I stayed at the Westin Harbour Castle. Unfortunately, after dining at the seafood buffet, I suffered a terrible bout of food poisoning that kept me in my hotel bed for two days. While management could not have been more accommodating throughout this ordeal, anyone who has been sick while travelling knows full well that you long for your own bed and room. During this time, I received a call from Langley GIS informing me that a contract had been placed on my life for the sum of ten thousand dollars.

Apparently, someone at a biker party spouted off that they would pay ten grand to kill me, and two individuals accepted the challenge. My wife was immediately moved to her parents and well-armed colleagues secured my home.

Upon my return the next day there was a meeting with a commanding officer, the detachment commander, members of GIS, and Staff Sergeant Jim Stinson, a long-time major crime investigator who had earned considerable respect relative to his organized-crime investigative abilities. Stinson dictated the way the threat would be handled. He felt launching a major crime investigation would take far too long and would expose me and my wife to prolonged danger. The method of dissipating the threat was simple: along with a couple of colleagues, I needed to go and confront the alleged conspirators. We were to firmly convey that we were aware of the threat and that if anything occurred, the wrath of the entirety of British Columbia's police resources would come down on them. I am not sure where I found the bravado to undertake this, but somehow, I was able to pull it off.

Maybe I have made this sound like just another day in policing. I can assure you this was not the case. It was terrifying for me. Lee and I had been married for less than a year and were living in a country home that we were in the process of fixing up. Her being sequestered with her parents, who also resided in Langley, did not give me a lot of comfort. And having armed members stay at our home weighed heavily on my psychological strength, or dare I say weakness.

We had the advantage of knowing the three individuals who'd agreed to carry out the alleged contract. I personally had had dealings with all of them during my tenure in the Langley Drug Section. Through intelligence, we deduced that they were capable of following through with the threat. It must be noted that at this time I was still dealing with the trials in Toronto, where there had also been a veiled threat; looking back, I am not sure that sending me east was the right call, but this was an era where you did not outwardly show fear.

Norm Leibel was assigned to go with me to visit each one of the suspect's homes for a heart-to-heart. Jim Stinson emphasized that if this was to work, I had to come across as being capable of more than they were. I vividly recall visiting the first location and having a conversation with two brothers who were allegedly involved. Given that I had dealt with them and knew them fairly well, we had what I can only describe as a "come to Jesus" meeting. It was made clear that if anything happened to me, my wife, or anything on my property, I would be back with a squad of officers, and that they'd better hope no one else was stupid enough to try something, because the blame would be on them and them alone.

We repeated this same scenario at a second location and by that time I was even more upset, getting fairly fired up, and would not tolerate any further threats. I am sure I sounded somewhat insane but that *was* the impression I wanted to leave behind. My false bravado worked, as a few weeks later when I was walking through Langley Bar, a group of bikers offered to buy me a beer, saying they had heard about how crazy I was. I have found myself wondering whether my approach was that sound; it really could have had the opposite effect.

A few months later there was an incident that involved my sports car. My wife worked at a car dealership in Langley, so she would drop me off at the department in our sports car and park it on the side of the road in front of the dealership. I was dropped off that evening and my wife went out to dinner. Later that evening, as we were driving together down the highway, the driver's-side front wheel came off and unfortunately we struck a car driven by a young lady. Although she was not injured, her car experienced massive damage. Someone had removed the lug nuts in my sports car, resulting in the wheel coming off. No suspects were ever identified, but it did give me cause for concern, and I am sure exacerbated my young wife's stress.

Chapter Seven

LANGLEY, BC, 1976–1978

DENNIS AND PATTY KNAPP

My partner at Langley from 1976–1978, Larry Campbell, later became a senator. Since we are both strong-willed, we did not always see eye to eye, but despite this, we were highly successful in our enforcement actions. Larry had a more in-depth knowledge of heroin traffickers than me, which exposed me to several higher-level cases, and our informants kept us extremely busy, which was good.

One interesting case we worked together involved a man by the name of Dennis Knapp and his wife, Patricia "Patty" Knapp, both now deceased. I knew Dennis and Patty well, as my wife had shown horses for them, and she and Patty were close friends. Dennis, whose family had left him considerable assets, mismanaged his money, and over the course of a few years, he turned to criminal activity to offset his spending habits. Around this time he was found to be involved in a large theft ring. The investigative team was aware that I knew both Dennis and Patty, so I was assigned to execute the warrant and make the arrests. At five in the morning, when I knocked on their trailer, Patty answered, her eyes still bleary from sleep, and invited me in. I explained the circumstances, and Patty told Dennis to get out of bed, because I was arresting them. Dennis said that since it was me, he would go peacefully. Patty made me a coffee prior to being taken into custody.

Sadly, a few years later, Dennis involved his sons in smuggling cocaine from the US, resulting in their arrest and conviction there. In March 1999, Patty and Dennis were murdered in their home in Vernon over a drug deal.

GARRY TAYLOR HANDLEN

In early 1977, an individual came to the Langley detachment and asked for me. He claimed to have extensive drug information. We met him and found him to have a criminal past—he was suspected of murdering a young girl in Matsqui, BC. I was able to get a copy of the psych evaluation and discovered he'd been labelled a psychopath with a likelihood of re-offending. Considering the risk this person posed, the criminal operations officer and chief superintendent, Bill Neale, reviewed the file. Since Handlen had expressed that he wanted to work with me, we agreed that I would continue to meet with the supposed psychopath and report all activity. The view was that this would help us keep tabs on him. Seeing as his information focused on some of the most notorious criminals in Vancouver, it was deemed well worth pursuing.

This man would prove to haunt me throughout my career. Although he initially provided relatively reliable drug information, I never, ever felt comfortable around him. I soon realized he had a side to him that was pure evil. In 1978 I came into the detachment in Langley and saw a composite drawing of a murder suspect in the Monica Rose Jack disappearance in Merritt. I immediately grabbed the drawing and asked what this person was suspected of doing. I contacted Corporal Doug Clyde, head of the GIS, and told him I believed that the suspect from the drawing was Handlen. Again, there is no such thing as a coincidence—Handlen had recently let me know he was headed to the BC Interior to fish and that he would driving a truck with a camper. This happened to be the suspect vehicle.

This information was relayed to the investigating staff sergeant in Kamloops, who came to Langley. I proposed that I call Handlen and ask for a meeting, since he always met with me without hesitation. For whatever reason, the staff sergeant chose to keep me on the sidelines. A raid was conducted on Handlen's residence, and it is my understanding that he was not home at the time. When he received knowledge of the raid (I believe he was tipped off by a friend), he fled to the US for a period.

The investigation failed to result in charges. As I was not involved, I cannot comment as to why; however, from day one, there was no doubt in my mind that Handlen was guilty. Although I never was able to investigate him myself, throughout my career I continued to push to have Handlen re-investigated. It was bittersweet when the RCMP cold-case squad contacted me in 2012 and asked for an overview of what I knew, since they had seen correspondence from me on the file. It was one of my happier days when he was arrested and charged in November 2014, as I felt this was unfinished business. I believed I had not done everything possible to bring this to fruition earlier, and so his subsequent conviction satisfied me—although it was forty years too late, justice was served.

My only hope is that he did not carry out any other murders while he was free.

Part Three

VANCOUVER DRUGS

Chapter Eight

HONING COLD APPROACHES
AMONG INTERESTING CHARACTERS

Shortly after the Handlen incident, I was moved to the Vancouver Drug Section where I worked on Unit 3 along with my former undercover partner Kim Marsh. Our unit was mandated to work on cocaine and chemical traffickers.

Working with the members of Vancouver Drugs was without a doubt one of the highlights of my career. Looking back on the members of the unit, I don't believe it would be possible to find a team of cops more egotistical and motivated than these. The level of competition among trained undercover operators served the section well, as we all continually tried to outdo each other. I am sure our leaders considered us a challenge. Many of us were young, ambitious, and inventive, therefore we never had to look for files to work on because someone always had something on the go. Many of these projects involved some form of undercover work. This unit helped me hone my ability to perform cold approaches. My inspiration was Geraldo Rivera, the American journalist who did several reports wherein he went undercover infiltrating criminal groups. My view was that law enforcement had better access to intelligence, so if a journalist could pull off a cold approach, it should be even easier for someone in the police milieu trained in undercover techniques. I found that the more inventive and elaborate the scheme, the more believable it was. Because of my success, I was asked to speak at undercover training courses explaining cold-approach techniques.

During one of these training sessions, the Vancouver "street crew" (a unit made up of RCMP and Vancouver drug-squad members assigned to work lower-level cases) provided me with a phone number belonging to an individual who had pounds of marijuana for sale. I was able to establish which bar he frequented. With the class of potential U/C operators observing, I demonstrated a cold approach on the phone. I contacted him and detailed a story about how I had gotten his contact information. I could not have had a more cooperative individual if I had provided him the script and told him to follow it. Surprise, surprise, we agreed to have him meet me in the parking lot of a hotel near the Vancouver International Airport as I explained that I had to fly back to Prince George on a five-p.m. flight. He showed up with over ten pounds of marijuana. During sentencing, the judge strongly recommended that the individual go into another career.

THE CHOIR GIRL

On another occasion we were working a project in the Abbotsford area and the local detachment asked if we would see about shutting down an individual who was moving cocaine out of a local bar. The detachment commander described the young female waitress named Teri who was trafficking the drug. The team agreed to see what we could uncover. A week or so later we were sitting in the bar having drinks with the waitress in question serving us. I asked her if there was anything else being served other than liquor. She asked, like what? Cocaine, I said. Teri seemed somewhat offended and did not bite on this occasion.

CHAPTER EIGHT

A week later I partnered with a female member and the two of us returned to the bar. Teri the waitress was serving, so I ordered drinks and apologized for embarrassing her the previous weekend with my directness. When she brought us our drinks, I asked if I could speak to her. When she sat down, I asked her what the "heat" situation was like. She replied that she was not sure about me. I responded, "Yeah, I'm a cop today and a motorcycle tomorrow." Teri laughed and wondered who had referred me to her. I replied that no one had, but as I saw that she seemed to know everyone, I'd assumed she would know some of the right people. I explained that I was from Toronto and had had a deal fall through the last time she saw me. She inquired if I would be moving out here to BC. I said I was in the process but had loose ends to tie up. Again I mentioned my business deal falling through, and she inquired if it was for "blow." Teri wanted to know whose fault it was that the deal fell through. I explained that the sample was excellent but when the supply arrived it was "the shits."

That's when Teri asked what I wanted. I told her I would purchase an ounce initially and more later, as I could not afford to risk a loss. She said the price was $2,200 an ounce. (For the record, all dollar amounts in this book, unless otherwise noted, are in Canadian dollars.) I told her the price was good, but I wanted a sample first. We agreed that a sample of one gram of untouched flake would be provided the next night for a hundred dollars.

The following night Constable McLean and I returned to the bar and had a couple of drinks, danced, and spoke with Teri. When she asked if I still wanted the sample, I replied in the affirmative. She said she'd forgotten it at home but was waiting for a friend to bring it. She returned later, stalling for more time, saying her friend brought the wrong sample. Shortly after midnight she came back to our table and we made our exchange—a hundred bucks for the sample—with an agreement that I contact her Monday to arrange the ounce if I was satisfied with the sample.

The following Monday, Teri and I made arrangements over the phone to meet at Sevenoaks Mall at one p.m. in front of Woodward's Food Floor. On Tuesday, the meeting occurred as arranged, and Teri suggested we go out to her car. We agreed to go to my rental vehicle and did the exchange for the ounce there. Teri had the cocaine in her purse. It was in a small baggie and was about the size of a golf ball. When I performed a touch test, I found the white substance oily when rubbed between my fingers. (If cocaine appears oily, and when placed in water completely dissolves, leaving an oily trail, it is likely pure cocaine, seeing as there is no residue to indicate a cutting agent, like milk sugar, was used.) I inquired what the cutting agent was, but Teri said she did not know, just that it came like this in small plastic bags from Florida. I floated the possibility that it was ephedrine, saying that a friend of mine had a "plug," so I used to use it. I also said I had a friend looking to score quantities of marijuana, as his supply had dried up. Teri implied she knew some people. I offered to introduce them, as I wanted nothing to do with pot—people talked too much. Teri agreed. We established that I would call her a week after I returned from Toronto.

A week later I called Teri. I told her I was still in Toronto but wanted to connect my friend looking for a supply of weed. She agreed to let me pass my friend her number.

About a week later I contacted the number Teri had provided and spoke to an unknown male. I left a message with him saying it was "Bobby" and that I wanted to meet Teri for lunch the following day at the Crossroads Restaurant. The next day I went to the Crossroads and called Teri, who agreed to come over immediately. She told me she had quit her job at the bar and going forward was managing large drug deals only. We discussed how her talks regarding the pot deal with her friend Dave were going, and she told me it was going well—she liked dealing with Dave. I spoke about a business acquaintance I had who would fund large deals and wondered about availability. Teri said the stuff I'd sampled was gone but that she had access to three pounds of flake (cocaine). She did some figuring on her place mat to figure out the price. Forty-eight ounces at $2,350 per ounce came to a total of $112,800. The price was too high, I said, and she needed to discuss a better one with her people. I explained that I was waiting to see if my property sold in Toronto; I had made good money selling antiques. I told her I would take a pound and then see if my friend would finance the other two.

As we ate lunch I let her know that I would need to get a price of $1,800 per ounce to make the deal financially viable for me. Teri agreed to speak to her people. I explained I would take as much as I could get, because the market in Toronto was dry. She left for a few minutes, and when she came back she handed me a folded paper, the size of a Wrigley's gum wrapper, containing a gram of cocaine. I said I would get back to her once I checked it.

At this point, we fully expected that she would introduce me to her brothers, known affiliates to an outlaw motorcycle gang. But you learn to expect the unexpected. This sample analyzed at virtual purity—nearly 100 percent cocaine. In our follow-up meeting to discuss the large deal, Teri showed up alone and said she was in a hurry to get to church choir. We discussed a three-pound deal, as this was all that was available, and agreed on a time and place to meet.

On the day of the deal, April 26, 1979, an investigative team set up early, and surprise of all surprises, Teri went to the location (a farmhouse between Abbotsford and Aldergrove), driving *all by herself* with no protection, picked up the three pounds, and drove to meet me in the parking lot with the drugs sitting *right there* on her front passenger seat. This was the first time I've witnessed this and the last time. Traffickers usually take far more precautions. This just goes to show how inexperienced Teri was.

Truly anything can occur when it comes to the criminal milieu. Although two others were charged along with the young waitress, she placed herself in the position of being one of the main organizers of the deal. In total, two pounds of cocaine were purchased using a flash roll, and eighteen more ounces were seized during searches, with a combined street value of seven hundred thousand dollars.

GOOD MORNING, MR. CLEMENT

Around this time, the drug project team started a major investigation involving John Vanderheide and his co-conspirators. I had previously investigated Vanderheide during my time in Langley, so he knew me well. The very first day the team's wiretap went live, on the first recorded call of the morning, Vanderheide started with something like, "Good morning, Mr. Clement, I hope you have a great day."

As you can imagine, there was some concern. My team was not sure what my relationship with him was. But I explained that this was daily routine with Vanderheide (which, for me, was a badge of honour). Each and every day when he woke up, as far as we could tell, Vanderheide would say good morning to me—I had gotten his attention over the years of my investigative files while stationed in Langley, after having earned a reputation among some of the major traffickers as a tenacious narc. I had confronted him on numerous occasions and believe some of the drugs that I was instrumental in seizing prior to this had emanated from him. I had clearly rattled his group in the past. Vanderheide likely thought this daily "good morning" was hilarious, not realizing we would get the last laugh.

HAWKEYE

Following the cocaine deal with Teri the waitress, I happened to be briefing my team on an individual who was dealing in multiple kilos of hashish near where we were working in the Abbotsford area. When I heard that his nickname was "Hawkeye," I realized I had met him in 1975 during an intelligence probe, an event I attended solely as eyes and ears for the investigative unit. I learned that he worked at a small service station, so I went to get some fuel. Lo and behold, out comes Hawkeye to pump the gas. I got out and let on that I was renewing our acquaintance. We immediately started discussing drugs, which ultimately led to an 8.5-pound purchase of hash and four arrests. But it wasn't exactly a piece of cake. When I gave the signal to take down the targets during the arrest, the individual who delivered the drugs, Hawkeye's buddy, realized something was amiss. This resulted in a fight and two broken ribs for me.

ABE

One of my section heads at that time was Staff Sergeant Abe Snidanko, a seasoned and well-respected drug officer who had been part of the Vancouver scene for years. In fact, he became so renowned for his drug arrests that Cheech Marin and Tommy Chong wrote a song about him. From the *Vancouver Sun*:

> Chong went on to make Grammy-winning comedy albums and movies, all with the stoner-comedy theme, often making fun of Sgt. Stadanko, a character based on a real-life Mountie narcotics officer named Abe Snidanko who prowled Fourth Avenue and busted people for drugs during the Summer of Love. "When [Snidanko] retired, his younger colleagues had me sign a poster for him," Chong recalls. "I don't think he's ever forgiven me."
>
> Snidanko, now retired and living in the Vancouver area, says he has forgiven Chong, but declined to talk about his drug squad days, saying: "I've been asked for interviews many times and I've refused everyone. And I'd like to keep it that way."[5]

Abe, due to his longevity in the world of drug traffickers, always kept our egos in check and put forward challenging expectations when we were working undercover on a target. On one occasion, Sergeant Ken Medford, Corporal Jim Tait, and I were trying to convince Abe to give us authorization for a flash roll so we could go through with a drug transaction, which would've resulted in an immediate arrest and retention of the funds. But because it required the approval of several levels of authority, and because the proposal came at the end of the week, Abe refused and instead challenged me to con the target without a flash roll. The meeting got quite heated, but Abe, in his calm fashion, remained steadfast. Unfortunately, I was not able to con the individual without showing some cash.

W.A.C. BENNETT DAM

Another interesting case I was assigned involved investigating a marijuana-dealing biker servicing Prince George and the surrounding area. To solidify my cover story, I was taken to the W.A.C. Bennett Dam (which was still under construction) to receive a bogus company identification as an electrician on location. After this I met with Walter Darbyson and negotiated a hundred-pound marijuana transaction. Darbyson was arrested. At the trial, his lawyer, Sid Simons, opted to make identification the main issue. Simons was familiar to us drug investigators as he represented many charged drug dealers and would resort to any number of antics to get a client off. The trial judge was known to be pro-police and the type of judge to demand decorum in his courtroom, so I took some liberties with the situation. When asked if I could identify Darbyson, I testified to the judge that Simons should be commended, since Mr. Darbyson's clean appearance and suit made for a total transformation of the defendant's personal style. I showed a picture of what Darbyson looked like at the time of his arrest to His Honour. Mr. Simons went ballistic at my insinuation that he was trying to deceive the court. Fortunately for me, His Honour agreed with me and severely verbally reprimanded Simons in open court for playing a game not allowed in his court. Each judge I appeared before had their own characteristics. The Prince George judge was a no-nonsense guy.

THE ANTIQUE SHOP

On another occasion, the project team was targeting a restaurant owner, Aristedes Pasparakis, alleged to be heavily involved in cocaine trafficking. Prior to concluding the file and recommending no further action be taken, I agreed to try a cold approach. Intelligence revealed that the target had been associating with a woman named "Carol" who had an antique shop near the restaurant. She had just moved from Hay River, Alberta, where she had owned another antique shop. I decided I'd attempt to go through Carol to get to the target. To prepare, I contacted the RCMP detachment in Hay River and obtained as much information as possible. The member I spoke to had, fortuitously, been in Carol's store and was able to describe it and the restaurant she often frequented.

Armed with this information, I visited her shop in Vancouver. As I was walking around the shop, I looked at Carol and feigned surprise that she was there, citing the "fact" that we had met in Hay River. As you can appreciate, running a shop open to the public, you meet hundreds of individuals, and so, like a good salesperson, she immediately acknowledged remembering me. Following this greeting we planned a lunch and drinks at the target's restaurant. Unfortunately for me and my team, the target was out of drugs at the time. No deal proceeded.

Chapter Nine

BEGINNING OF THE 1980 VANCOUVER UNDERCOVER OPERATION

I was approached by Staff Sergeant Hugh Stewart (corporal at the time) and Staff Sergeant Mike Butcher (constable at the time) and asked if I would go undercover for a minimum six-month project. The previous operator opted out at the eleventh hour, so, with all the legwork done and an informant already in Vancouver ready to introduce an operator, they were stuck. I decided to discuss it with my wife that evening and get her opinion before committing.

Well, Lee agreed. She felt that since I had already been involved in ongoing undercover operations periodically since 1978, it may as well be formalized. Upon reviewing the targets, I realized there were a few that I had dealt with as a drug officer, so after discussions with the two officers, Superintendent Lyman Henschel and Inspector Dick Dickens (later assistant commissioner), I dyed my hair, got a set of glasses with photochromic transition lenses, and grew a goatee.

Before delving into the details of this operation, I would be remiss if I did not comment on my respect for both Lyman and

Dick. As I rose through the ranks, these two individuals, along with Assistant Commissioner Rod Stamler, were mentors for me, and leaders whom I hope to say I emulated to the greatest degree possible. Lyman remained in Vancouver where he oversaw the drug section for many years and, in my view, showed what a great police leader was all about. Dick went to Ottawa and over the years rose to the assistant commissioner level. Assistant commissioners generally act as the commanding officers of each division, though they can also be found in HQ overseeing certain areas. I had the pleasure of following Dick to Ottawa following the Vancouver undercover operation, for reasons that will become evident shortly.

THE TEAM

The Vancouver undercover operation team consisted of the following people:

- Superintendent Lyman Henschel, RCMP, Officer in Charge (OIC) Drug Enforcement Branch
- Inspector Lloyd Smith, RCMP, OIC Drug Support Services
- Staff Sergeant Dennis Smith, RCMP, Non-commissioned OIC Undercover Operations
- Staff Sergeant Hugh Stewart, RCMP, Operation Lead
- Constable Garry Clement, RCMP, Cover
- Staff Sergeant Mike Butcher, RCMP, Cover
- Detective Gary Dalton, Vancouver Police, Cover
- Constable Ray Peach, RCMP, Cover
- Sergeant Jim Ballantyne, RCMP
- Corporal Barry Bennett, RCMP

This operation provided me an education in that it was the first time I fully appreciated the impact of heroin addiction, the toll addiction takes on society and individuals, and the sophistication of organized crime. The operation required that I frequent the Blackstone Hotel, where many mid-level heroin traffickers and addicts hung out. I witnessed addicts' daily routines, as they came together at least twice a day to buy their next "fix."

As I said, the Blackstone Hotel at Davie and Granville was home to mid-level traffickers and a population of addicts. It was the hotel where connections were made, and many addicts went there to score their required fixes. To fit in, I would need to be accepted by the patrons of the hotel, many of whom were well associated in the drug trade. This hotel is where the Vancouver undercover operation commenced. Many of the patrons who frequented the hotel, some of whom had been at one time high-level criminals, started vouching for me as someone who was connected on the East Coast.

From the early 1900s through to the 1970s, the hotel was known as the Martinique, but during the 1970s it was renamed the Blackstone, before becoming the Hotel California for Expo 86. For a time, it was on the list of single-room occupancy hotels. Then, in the late 1990s, after a major makeover, the hotel became a Howard Johnson's.

I witnessed firsthand several young ladies who would do anything for that next dose of heroin, and how they were mistreated by pimps. Two ladies really hit this home for me. Vicky was a tall blonde who had become hooked on heroin at an early age. While I was undercover in Vancouver, she was selling sex; at one point she went aboard a Colombian freighter while it was in port. She was held for days on the ship. When she was released, she had to be hospitalized. Those on the ship had beaten her so badly it resulted in some permanent disabilities. Since she was a known addict and prostitute, no one undertook any sort of investigation. I learned that she was considered somewhat lucky; she could have been hauled out to sea and dropped overboard.

There was a second young lady I knew who was severely addicted and became pregnant. Since I'd passed myself off as a non-user and treated the women with respect, when I was in the Blackstone they often would sit, have a beer with me, and confide in me. In fact, they talked openly on the street about me being their protector (by this time I had built a reputation as being someone well connected from "back east")—which even came to the attention of the Vancouver PD and the RCMP street investigative team. I asked her directly how she could go through with having the child. She said, with tears in her eyes, that this was the only event in her life now allowing her to feel like a human being and a woman.

I have never forgotten that conversation. These events strengthened my resolve to take as many high-level traffickers as possible off the street and to focus on organized crime. I recognized that people at those levels would do anything for money. I also realized that traffickers and organized crime preyed upon the street addicts. The women I saw on the street, too focused on their next fix to seek to liberate themselves, were being financially exploited by their pimps. After thirty years, law enforcement and some politicians have finally started to recognize that street addicts are just victims, but without the necessary support for addiction, the strategy of "safe supply" will result in dismal failure.

The Blackstone Hotel operation would not have been successful if not for the information gathered during my previous Toronto operation, wherein I was regaled to—story after story—about the famous Toronto Homicide officers Nicolucci and Barbetta. Barbetta's reputation was legendary. Feared by bank robbers, loved and admired by police officers and citizens, his thirty-two-year career ended in 1985 at the rank of staff superintendent while in charge of the No. 5 District, the largest and most coveted command in the Metropolitan Toronto Police. Working details of their alleged arrest activities into my "from back east" story had given me a tremendous advantage.

This assignment began on March 17, 1980, and terminated on September 10, 1980. As a result, forty-six persons were charged with seventy offences under the Narcotic Control Act (now called the Controlled Drugs and Substances Act).

The goal of the Blackstone project was to be introduced, with the help of informant and agent Doug White (now deceased), into some of the highest levels of the criminal milieu in Vancouver. Doug had served time back east for his drug-trafficking activities and had previously been very active trafficking in Vancouver. With the restrictions now in existence for informants, this method of operation would not be possible today, since today Doug would be classified as an agent (which would mean he would have to testify). An informant provides information but does not take direction from police. Though we termed Doug an informant back then, he was under our direction and essentially acted for us. The reality was, following the arrests, who he was and what he did for us became publicly known and therefore concealing his identity was not even possible. There is no doubt that during the operation he was using cocaine and also putting out heroin. The fact that Doug shared with his contacts that I was his partner in crime and the fact that drugs purchased by Doug hit the street generated massive credibility for my U/C persona, but in today's environment, strict controls would need to be placed on Doug, and it would be necessary to seek preapproval from the Crown for any activity that breaches the law.

At the time, Vancouver was a hub for heroin and cocaine, and home to organized criminals with strong ties to prominent Italian-based organized-crime figures, so management continually sought out opportunities to use undercover operators, with the help of informants, to infiltrate the Vancouver crime world.

Having worked in Vancouver prior to the operation was somewhat of a bonus. I had already heard about or read about many of the targets in case files. Some of them were mentioned in Jean-Pierre Charbonneau's book *The Canadian Connection* (also published by Optimum Publishing International), including Rolland Trudel, Stan Lowe, Gordon Kravenia, all of whom were connected to Italian organized crime in Montreal through Bob Tremblay, a former Vancouver trafficker and bodybuilder.

My very first buy was an ounce of heroin arranged through Whytie Jacobs, a sixty-four-year-old long-time criminal connected to Rolland Trudel and many other criminal elites. Unfortunately, the heroin was anything but heroin, and since this was a first buy, it was essential to ensure the loss was reimbursed or the bogus heroin replaced. This meant I had to put word out on the street that I was looking to speak to Whytie. About a week later I was given a heads-up that he was in a Chinese restaurant down from the Blackstone.

To show I was serious and not a person to take advantage of, I went into the restaurant and spoke to Whytie, feigning I was livid and threatening to take his knees off with a baseball bat if he couldn't make up the loss. Although it sounds harsh, as I testified in court, Whytie's connections made my threat not much of a threat (had he really been concerned, he could've had them retaliate), but it served to give me credibility and an eventual meeting with Rolland Trudel.

Trudel was well known within the heroin trade and connected to William Faulder "Fats" Robertson, a Vancouver gang leader. Robertson was a known associate of Robert "Bob" Tremblay, who'd served a twenty-year sentence in 1955 for heroin importation. In a meeting in Montreal following Tremblay's release in 1969, Tremblay and Trudel were observed meeting with associates of Lucien Rivard, a major heroin importer well connected with Montreal Italian organized crime.

The meeting between Whytie, Trudel, and I proved interesting. It was evident that Trudel was extremely cautious and concerned about dealing with someone he did not know. Despite this, we reached an agreement; I would either be repaid $1,600 or receive a half ounce of quality heroin this time around. Trudel was anything but talkative. Whytie later explained to me that despite the fact

Trudel knew I was not a "bull," seeing no cop would threaten like I did, and since I had been vouched for, the man remained cautious and did not want to deal directly with me.

MY VOUCHERS

At the Blackstone Hotel around the same time, an addict and trafficker named Mim Gendron started telling people she knew who my brother was from back east and could vouch for my criminal family ties. I never elaborated on her claims—I'll never know why she felt she knew my family or at least felt compelled to say that she did, whether it was an outright lie or a false belief—but they helped provide me credibility in the criminal community.

During a subsequent meeting, Mim established that both she and Trudel were connected in Montreal. She kept me in the loop regarding the replacement heroin Trudel owed me. She also shared with me that the people in Montreal were unhappy with Trudel because he owed them a substantial amount of money. It seemed Trudel was trying to rely on his past relationship with Bob Tremblay. She claimed to have given him $34,000 but only received four ounces of heroin, which was garbage. It was understood that the link in Montreal was going to handle this problem.

Even though Mim, Kravenia, Whytie, and Doug White vouched for me, Trudel never agreed to meet directly with me again, but he did ensure that a half ounce was given to me for the poor-quality ounce. Mim applied pressure to her people in Montreal to force Rolly Trudel to begin dealing heroin to me, to no avail, perhaps due to the money owed by Trudel.

Several weeks later, Whytie came through with another half ounce of superior-quality heroin. It was laid down in a cigarette package (which was the way the Montreal-connected suppliers operated). Whytie went with me to get the package and during the ride to the location, he asked if I could get some empty #5 capsules, as he had some capping to do. This was an aspect of the operation that worked well, as those who sought empty capsules, like Whytie, used them to create bundles of heroin for street sale, thereby providing intelligence for the drug sections on who was dealing at street level. (When asked in court what we did with the funds from the capsules, I explained that the money went to our end-of-operation party. His Honour replied that he was sorry he'd missed it.)

At a later meeting with Whytie at the Blackstone Hotel, he informed me that he spoke with Kravenia, who had vouched for me; there would be no further issues regarding my bona fides and he would pass this on to Trudel. Following Whytie's arrest he was sentenced to Matsqui Institution, a federal medium-security prison, where it so happened my father-in-law was an upholstery instructor. Whytie enrolled in the course and explained to my father-in-law how a young cop had duped some high-level criminals.

Being a relatively new face in a criminal milieu raises all kinds of questions. Having Doug White introducing us helped, but it did not satisfy the more organized criminals. Fortunately, my vague "from back east" story and my narrative that I was proving to my family that I could manage things out west seemed to resonate, and some individuals, like Mim, helped out by commenting that they knew who my family was. I also stated that I had been active in Vancouver in the seventies and somehow, two respected and long-time crim-inals, Gord Kravenia and Stanley Lowe (who were, according to Jean-Pierre Charbonneau, author of *The Canadian Connection,* "two of the most active heroin distributors on the Canadian west coast in 1960"), indicated they remembered me. Their endorsement was better than Doug White's due to their esteemed status with higher-level individuals and on the street. Although I never did any dealings directly with Kravenia or Lowe, we were often seen having a drink together at the Blackstone Hotel. They continued to vouch for me and, following the end of the operation and the arrests, Kravenia called Superintendent Lyman Henschel and said that he felt my performance merited an Oscar—high praise coming from someone who had been part of the criminal milieu for decades.

Dealing with some of the most notorious criminals in Vancouver provided an understanding of the criminal mindset analogous to the kind of education you get with a graduate degree. Once assimilated, you become part of a unique group, considered by many a trusted colleague, and respected to a degree by some of the lower-level criminals. Regardless, as a newcomer you have to be careful and constantly vigilant. I continually stated that if someone did not trust me, there were no hard feelings and certainly no need to feel pressure to go through with any drug transaction. This helped solidify my reputation. I always expressed to whomever I was meeting and potentially dealing with that I would be checking them out and they were free to do the same with me.

Shortly after embarking on the operation, I was seated at the Blackstone in the bar area with a group of addicts and traffickers. As was customary for the time, the "street crew" police team came into the bar and began questioning some of the patrons. I was a new face, so they grabbed me and hauled me into the washroom. Detective Jens Lind recognized me as an officer once he got me in the washroom. He commented that my new hair colour had changed my appearance. It gave me comfort to not be immediately recognized by Jens, since I'd worked the streets previously. At this time the street drug investigators were fairly heavy-handed and did not hesitate to push around a suspected dealer, so I had Jens hit me in the face. I bled a little. When I returned to the table, the fact that I was roughed up gave me tremendous credibility and the group eased up on any further questioning into my background.

Chapter Ten

SOME OF THE MORE INTERESTING TRANSACTIONS

THE PENTHOUSE CABARET

Any criminals active in Vancouver from the fifties to the late eighties knew the Penthouse Cabaret well. Many business personnel and criminals frequented this bar in the evenings, Thursday through Saturday. The Penthouse was located on 1019 Seymour Street, and in the early years was known as an afterhours hangout for patrons and performers who wanted to carry on the party from other local clubs. The Penthouse had originally been a boxing club named Eagle Time Athletic Club. It was owned by Joe Filippone and it served as a place for young boxers to practice during the day. At night, however, Filippone hosted large afterhours parties in the upstairs "penthouse" section. These parties grew so popular and regular that Joe decided to move into the nightclub business legitimately, naming his establishment "The Penthouse."

The Penthouse grew a reputation as an infamous strip club, with many of the strippers featured in *Penthouse* magazine. Because of frequent criminal associations, the club also was famous for murders.

Entertainers from Ella Fitzgerald to Sting to Frank Sinatra hung out at the Penthouse, and it was the background for many movies and TV shows.

The Penthouse was also a meeting place for high-priced prostitutes and therefore under constant surveillance by Vancouver PD. There were rumours that city council members, stockbrokers, provincial politicians, and Supreme Court judges had been photographed there. The tape recorders had captured phone calls in which gambling and money deals were discussed. One police officer said the growing file was "a blackmailer's dream." The police department classified many of the photographs, and what happened to them after all these years is described in Aaron Chapman's 2013 book *Liquor, Lust, and the Law: The Story of Vancouver's Legendary Penthouse Nightclub*.

In 1983, not three years after my undercover operation ended, seventy-year-old Joe Filippone was gunned down in his office on the night of September 18. "At the end of the day . . . two people were convicted of a robbery and they both got twenty-five years in prison."[6] More than eight hundred people showed up to Filippone's funeral, a crowd described as "Supreme Court justices, businessmen, and dancers."

To be noticed by many of the criminal who's who, it was necessary to be part of the "in" group at the Penthouse Cabaret and to be visibly friendly with Joe Filippone. After a few months undercover, I was taken to the club by a woman who was well-known amongst the upper echelons of the criminal milieu, Jan Thibodeau. Jan was an addict who'd been in the drug scene for years and was widely considered a friend by prominent traffickers despite being a heroin user. An intro from her was as good as gold. Plus, my supposed "back east" ties and my supposed former connection to Gord Kravenia had started to circulate, which made acceptance among the more notable criminals much easier to achieve. In a single evening, I was introduced to some of the more notorious Vancouver criminals at that time: Cliff Baldwin and Mervin Kroll, in company of Eddie Cheese (a.k.a. Eddie Young). I was also given a VIP pass to the Penthouse by Joe Filippone and a second one to the Crazy Horse by Mervin Kroll. This particular event cemented my persona as genuine and ensured my ongoing undercover success with Filippone and the others. That night I matched Cheese round for round in drink purchases. He'd initially tried to see if I would spring for all the drinks, something other undercover operators were apparently known to do. Instead, I told him not to be so cheap, and that I would match him round for round instead. The bill that evening amounted to several hundred dollars and required some explaining.

EDDIE CHEESE

My first introduction to Cheese was by chance. Doug and I were out meeting other potential suppliers when Cheese happened to drive by us. He drove up to my vehicle, Doug spoke to him, and we agreed to meet at the Playfair. The Playfair Club was an out-of-the-way gambling establishment off Davie, which was tightly controlled and monitored by the criminal patrons, such as Yogi Cameron, a well-known drug trafficker highly respected by many of the criminal upper echelon (and decidedly *not* the model and wellness ambassador of the same name). Montreal-connected organized-crime groups frequently gambled in the club. Cameron was often seen with Danny and Paul Sectley, who had served time for attempting to "finish the job" on someone they beat up while the subject was being operated on at the Royal Columbian Hospital in New Westminster. The cover team told me that I needed to be extremely careful around the Sectley brothers as the word on the street was they would not hesitate to shoot a person. Whether this was true or not, I can say that when I entered the Playfair, Danny was anything but friendly, and certainly went out of his way to make me feel uncomfortable. He left no doubt in my mind that if he had assumed I was a cop, I would've paid a heavy price. Looking back, the Playfair Club was one of the most stressful locations I was required to attend. Each time I went, I ensured I had an exit planned, if required.

That first night I met Cheese, when we got to Playfair's parking lot, Cheese came over to my vehicle. Doug introduced me as his partner and proceeded to point out a necklace Cheese was wearing, saying he was going to buy it from him next week. Cheese asked if either of us wanted to buy a new Longines watch valued at $500 to $600 for $250. Doug said he would take it, so Cheese went to his car and returned with a brown case containing the watch.

After this, we had several meetings at the Penthouse and Crazy Horse that made it much easier to arrange higher-level deals with the who's who. Eddie Cheese had been an ongoing target due to his previous civil action against the RCMP for what he argued was a false arrest, and for his ensuant ability to avoid charges. We met with him on a few occasions. In one of our meetings, he disconcertingly explained how several RCMP undercover operators had tried to arrange a deal with him. He even named the officers. When he articulated this, I went on the offensive and said he was too much of a target and I didn't want to be seen around him. This obviously struck a nerve with him; he trusted me enough to meet with me a few more times. On one of these occasions I asked him if he knew anyone who could unload a truckload of furs that had been stolen in a heist. Over the next hour, he taught me how to remove dye-lot numbers on furs and assured me of his commitment that when the time was right, he could arrange it. Flowing from this, Cheese sold me a silver-plated .45, as he heard I might need some protection, and eventually a quarter pound of cocaine. As a fitness nut who was extremely health conscious, Cheese was unlike many of the other criminals, but he was well connected and had been deemed dangerous by the RCMP.

During these meetings, my knowledge of the alleged actions of Toronto detectives Nicolucci and Barbetta paid off. In one meeting,

Cheese and I discussed how Nicolucci and Barbetta loved to make arrestees walk into Lake Ontario in the middle of winter. Cheese felt that if I had survived the wrath of these detectives, I had to be solid.

In one of my meetings with Cheese, he inquired if I would invest in a pound of pure heroin with him. He had access to it in Los Angeles, but since the price was eighty thousand dollars, he wanted to have a couple other investors. Cheese apparently had a trucker friend who would transport it, as he was in the States every week. At this same meeting Cheese wanted to know if I could move some 2.5-carat diamonds. I received the .45 revolver at this meeting. Cheese explained he wore boots all the time in order to carry his .38. At a subsequent meeting we discussed the LA trip again but both agreed that we needed to transact a few more deals locally to build a nest egg.

In one of my meetings with Cheese, he said he could arrange a meeting for me with Sonny Barger, the founding member of the Oakland chapter of the Hells Angels Motorcycle Club. I discussed this with the cover team and the senior officers, but it was deemed too risky from a cover point of view to explore further. That being said, this offer clearly demonstrated that things were going well for my undercover work in Vancouver.

At this same meeting I ran into Yogi Cameron, who warned me I needed to be careful as my name was surfacing on the Vancouver PD scanners. He also spoke of his meeting at the Blackstone Hotel with Bobby Johnson, who later turned up dead—executed. It is noteworthy that at one of my prior meetings, I encountered Bobby Johnson socializing with several individuals I had been dealing with over several months. Bobby, who I now can safely say was an RCMP informant, came up to me and wanted to know how things were going. After bouncing back and forth a few times, with me feigning like I didn't know what he was talking about, he came right out with it and said that he knew who I was and what my assignment was. I wasn't sure what his intentions were, so I quickly told him that I knew he was an informant who worked with Sergeant Lloyd Neville. While I was unnerved somewhat by his knowledge of my assignment, the fact that I knew his relationship with Neville obviously shocked him. We agreed we both had a lot to lose if either of us revealed anything. Bobby wished me luck and he stayed clear of me for the rest of the operation. Information about who was behind his execution never surfaced during my time remaining undercover, but the rumour and discussions amongst high-level criminals linked it to the drug trade. I strongly suspect he'd been linked to being a source, but this is purely speculation.

Toward the end of the project, Yogi Cameron and later Reece Sutherland had warmed to me. Both were thought to be tied to Bob Tremblay, described by Jean-Pierre Charbonneau in *The Canadian Connection* as Lucien Rivard's lieutenant. (Rivard was a major heroin trafficker and importer in the late fifties and sixties.) Tremblay was originally from Vancouver and set out to manage the West Coast heroin trade. He later returned to Montreal, but maintained ties in Vancouver through Rolland Trudel, Cameron, and Sutherland.

PAUL LEVINSON AND DEBRA CHONG

One of the heroin purchases was analyzed as the highest-purity heroin we'd seen in many years. As a result, a subsidiary investigation was launched that discovered the source of the supply and resulted in arrests by one of the other project teams. One of the main targets was a close associate of Barry Ackerman's, who in 1979 was arrested in Thailand with seven hundred grams of heroin. Ackerman got life in prison, though at that time, a hundred grams of heroin under Thailand's tough drug laws carried the death penalty. Over the course of several meetings, Paul Levinson and his girlfriend, Debra Chong, explained to me how they were sending money over to Thailand so that Ackerman could get decent food.

Levinson and Chong were heavily into dealing cocaine at that time and were heavy users.

During a purchase at Orestes Restaurant on July 25, 1980, I met with Levinson, Chong, and Mervin Kroll after having negotiated a one-ounce sample deal of cocaine with Levinson and Chong. As we waited for the ounce, Chong explained that she and Levinson were connected to Barry Ackerman, and that he'd been busted in Thailand—"fingered" by a mule—resulting in her having to flush an ounce of "blow" and an ounce of "stuff" (heroin), and that an additional six ounces of "stuff" disappeared after the arrest. She further explained that since Ackerman's arrest, she and Levinson had spent about $150,000 trying to help him and were sending five hundred dollars per month for his living expenses in jail. But, she said, lately things had been tough, so she hadn't been able to send the usual five hundred, and Ackerman was now complaining that he'd come down with a bad skin rash and had no money to get treatment. She also told me that they were planning something that should secure his freedom within six months.

Mervin Kroll had some cocaine, and he offered a "snort" to the table. Levinson and another unknown party immediately took him up on his offer. He offered some to me, so I placed it on my thumb and simulated use. I ended up with some powder on the side of my face, so Mervin gave me a lesson on how to hold the cocaine on my thumb properly. No one got wise to the fact that it was due to my feint that I got the cocaine on my face.

The day ended up with only a quarter-ounce sample purchase of cocaine but paved the way for future deals, and solidified my relationship with some well-documented higher echelon traffickers and importers. I also learned through Chong that Levinson's cocaine connection was part of the Fats Robertson organization. Robertson had been sentenced to twenty years in jail in 1978 for conspiracy to traffic in $3.5 million in cocaine, along with fourteen other co-conspirators. Chong explained that Levinson and Robertson's associate got her started in the business five years earlier by fronting her a pound of cocaine.

LARRY BECK

The deal with Larry Beck turned out to be a disconcerting one. Beck had access to cocaine and heroin, allegedly from Barry Ackerman's contacts, and agreed to an initial one-ounce cocaine transaction, which required fronting the money to his contact. Fronting money was somewhat taboo in the RCMP, but refusing to do so was a recognized tell for a narc—it was common knowledge that cops did not front. Well, Beck's supplier did not return when promised. I told Beck that he would pay for any loss one way or another. He had me drive to the supplier's residence. He went into the house and came out a few minutes later with a woman he referred to as the supplier's "old lady." They both got in my vehicle, and he told her that she would suffer long before he did. I immediately reassured her I only wanted to get my money from her husband or get the drugs. In the end, the supplier, John Martin, returned and provided the ounce, apologizing for the rush as he had to drive to a location farther away.

THE INFAMOUS DOUG PAYNE

During the latter stages of that undercover operation, I linked with another operator who had been working with an agent at a much higher level. Staff Sergeant Doug Payne was much older that I was and therefore more readily welcomed by some of the upper echelon criminals. A discussion ensued with my cover team and superiors. We agreed that to entrench myself with some of the Mafia-connected traffickers, I should use Doug Payne's U/C name as a reference, if and when required. At this time, I was still trying to fully ingratiate myself with Cameron and Sutherland, so I gave

Payne's name as a reference. Unbeknownst to me, Staff Sergeant Payne told Sutherland that he didn't know me, which was a big surprise and a bit of setback. I contacted Payne and, after some very colourful language on my part regarding his lack of reference, he commented that he had full faith in me that I would be able to talk my way around this. Payne was killing himself laughing at the time. I was glad one of us found this funny. But, like Payne said, we move forward and adapt.

REECE SUTHERLAND

If you ever saw Reece Sutherland on the street, you would probably think he was a respectable businessman. He dressed well and treated drug dealing as you would any business, with one exception: he was cognizant of the risks and took every precaution to satisfy himself that deals would not lead to his arrest. Prior to agreeing to a quarter-pound heroin transaction, Reece demanded to speak with Doug White, the agent/source who by this time had been relocated. It was decided to fly Doug in from Alberta and arrange a meeting at the Vancouver International Airport.

Sutherland showed up that day at the airport with his wife and two children. Once he was satisfied that it was safe to have a discussion, his wife and children left, and Reece first met privately with Doug and then with me, at which time we reached an agreement to proceed with the quarter-pound heroin purchase. The drugs were to be concealed in an alley and the address would be provided upon payment.

A day later, we picked up the heroin stash following direction from Reece. My team and I agreed this would be the last purchase and the end of the operation, with arrests scheduled to occur early the next morning.

Chapter Eleven

THE PURLOINED LETTER

At about the four-month mark of this new operation it was revealed that a report had been stolen out of a police courier vehicle. This report had the potential to reveal my undercover role, and so the case was nicknamed "the Case of the Purloined Letter" because of it. It listed full details about my identity and activities as an infiltrator in the underworld. As anyone who has seen television shows involving organized crime might imagine, the concerns about this went all the way to the senior command in British Columbia. A criminal operations officer even met with me to discuss any safety concerns I might have.

Panic ensued for a couple days. We felt the operation may be compromised. In the end, the decision whether to continue or not was left to me. After discussion with the team, I agreed to continue, but we doubled the size of the cover team and decided that I needed to start packing a firearm. I was trained to handle a Walther PPK 9mm, which I then carried throughout the remainder of the operation. All future meetings with our targets were well planned out with ample backup at the ready in the event of the report information surfacing.

Even with these precautions, though, the level of stress I was under from this point on bordered on unbearable. I had always operated under the assumption that a conviction for drug trafficking was a far cry from a conviction for the murder of a police officer, and that if the criminal target was willing to meet and carry out a drug transaction, then it was highly doubtful I would be discovered. I also was familiar enough with the targets to know that, although at least some of them were capable of murder, it was low on the probability scale that they would pursue a cop.

This view was not unanimous. That is the reason the final decision fell to me. I think this was the one time in my career that I was not entirely honest with my wife, which likely reflected that, subconsciously, I was not completely certain that continuing with the operation was the right move. Following this theft of my info, whenever I had to go into a location to meet someone, I am sure my blood pressure was in borderline stroke territory. This was likely the reason Doug White (the agent) and I would start the day with a double Scotch.

Fortunately, the rest of the operation continued without incident and we carried out further major buys of heroin. It was finally decided that the operation had plateaued, therefore a final quarter pound of heroin was ordered with the decision to make arrests the next morning. After finishing up with the operation for the day, the cover team and I met at an RCMP member's home and celebrated our success. This was definitely not a bright move, seeing as we had to be somewhat functioning by five a.m. for the arrests and searches.

Relying on many members of Vancouver Drugs and the Vancouver Police Department, the arrests and searches occurred simultaneously early the next morning. Each target was brought to the police cells where I was re-introduced to them as a police officer. Reaction varied, but many seemed to accept the ramifications of their actions, especially some of the more notable targets. It went like this: Each of the accused was brought into a booking room and identified as the individual I had dealt with. Then I was introduced by my real title and a photo was taken of the two of us. Looking at the photos now it is clear I had too much to drink the night before; I looked worse than the arrestees.

In correspondence with Superintendent Henschel, retired chief superintendent Bill Neale described the operation as "the most successful undercover operation in this district insofar as the stature and level of traffickers apprehended." The quote later appeared in my evaluation and was the impetus for my receiving a commendation and a Lieutenant Governor's Award from the Province of British Columbia.

Following the operation, unnamed members in the Vancouver Drug Section are said to have made allegations against the undercover team and myself, leading to two internal investigations. The allegations were that I had been stopped for impaired driving, that my U/C rental car had been damaged and the damage never reported, and that the cover team failed to maintain professionalism during the operation. All of these allegations were found to be unsupported by any evidence. Far too often, professional jealousy was present. By the way, if the allegations had proven true, they would not have impacted the operation or court proceedings, as the information pursued was weak. This all goes to show how petty some members can be when another team achieves success. I was fortunate that the officers in HQ's drug branch took a firm position, which led to the file being concluded.

Part Four

STARTING AT HEADQUARTERS

Chapter Twelve

THE CALL

Although it had always been cited as a possibility that my wife and I would need to be transferred out of the division in Vancouver, reality never set in until a transfer was recommended, in which Superintendent Lyman Henschel wrote:

> There is no question this member has reason to be concerned for his safety. The stature of the criminals he has brought before the courts needs no additional comment from me other than to say that in my view, they included some of the most dangerous figures in this city.

I was given two options, Alberta or Headquarters. As Inspector Dick Dickens, former officer with Vancouver Drugs (and one of the cops who'd advised me to change my appearance prior to the undercover operation), had transferred to Ottawa and was someone I greatly respected, I opted to go to Ottawa after consulting with my wife, believing this would be a great move.

Unfortunately, it did not turn out to be a normal transfer. The investigators learned that there'd been an alleged contract taken out on me and it was deemed urgent to move Lee and I immediately. We picked her up at work and let her know that she would not be able to return. We then travelled to Ottawa to look for a new home while the force managed the sale of her BC home. We had Lee's horse, so this required us to drive with a horse trailer and seek out boarding facilities upon arrival in Ottawa.

At this time there were no support systems in place for stress, and no actual program that dealt with security for members. Although Dickens was a solid operational officer and fully understood the impact the alleged contract was having on me, and although my soon-to-be new boss Rod Stamler was exceptional in providing what support he could, actual programs were sadly lacking.

We located a home in the country, since we would be relocating one of our horses with us (the other horse had to be quickly sold). Upon arrival in Ottawa in late November, we started preparing our new home, including cleaning the carpets. On her way to go rent a carpet cleaner, Lee was broadsided by another vehicle, tremendously damaging our vehicle and shaking her up badly. Our furniture arrived and it is that evening that I received the call from Hugh Stewart detailed in the introduction to this book: that the alleged threat had followed us to Ottawa. He wanted me to get a firearm, load it, go to the nearest OPP detachment immediately, and call him.

I cannot adequately explain the thoughts flowing through my mind. The guilt I felt for bringing this onto my spouse hung over me and has never really disappeared. When I called from the detachment, they explained that they'd received what they believed to be credible information: that two hit men out of Montreal had met with some of the more notorious criminals in Vancouver and agreed to take the contract. As the prosecutor's office told the court I was moved to Ottawa for security reasons, the investigators believed I was no longer safe in my new city.

As my sister was down helping with the unpacking, I loaded everyone into the rental vehicle with some hastily packed clothes and drove into Ottawa looking for the OPP station. We were new to the city, so we didn't know our way around, nor did we have a lot of contacts. Today it would seem borderline crazy for an officer under threat to have to carry a loaded shotgun and drive his family, unescorted, to a police station. It simply isn't professional, or safe. And I know, as I did share my thoughts with him, that this is what the duty sergeant thought as well. The prudent response would have been for an emergency response team to come to the house and escort me and my family to a secure location.

Finding a motel was the next issue. I wanted to ensure, for greater protection, that we had a room with a good view of the parking lot. Vancouver was convinced the threat was real and had come from some of the organized-crime figures I'd purchased drugs from and who had allegedly carried out contract killings. It was a good thing I wasn't anything but a social drinker at this time, as I am sure I could have gone down a very dark path.

The next day I met with Wayne Blackburn, a friend from Vancouver who was now stationed in Headquarters. He suggested I move in with my parents in Elmira for a few weeks until more facts could be determined once the investigation was launched. Although this initially seemed like a good idea, it turned out to be anything but. Shortly after arriving at my parent's home in Kitchener, the RCMP showed up. They briefed me on potential concerns and how they would ensure a response if required. This weighed heavily on me, as I realized that I now had involved my parents into my work. This was a rookie mistake—it should never have been considered until the seriousness of the threat had been fully evaluated. We should have been under protection until the threat was fully resolved.

How this affected me was best articulated in the *Globe and Mail*. Reporter Peter Moon received permission from Headquarters to interview me in 1981. Allow me to paraphrase that interview: There was a year where my house outside of Ottawa was alarmed like Fort Knox. Every time there was a fluctuation in the power current (living in a rural setting, this happened occasionally), the alarm would go off and I'd have an Ontario Provincial Police cruiser arrive with two guys bouncing out of the car with shotguns. I became disillusioned and began increasing my consumption of alcohol. My blood pressure went up and my doctor told me to stop drinking. I was going through a terrible time, but Lee saved me. I'd start to drink, and she would tell me to smarten up. After a time, I put a halt to the excessive drinking. I said enough is enough, I've got to get back to a normal life. If somebody wants to shoot me, all the alarms in the world are not going to stop it. I started running instead, eventually building up to over five miles a day.

Reflecting back, it is no wonder so many undercover and plain-clothes members end up with alcohol problems. We were not to complain about stress or indicate that we were hurting in any way. We were expected to get back to the task at hand. Fortunately today, stress and PTSD are becoming better understood and acknowledged as a potential reality of the job. I would argue there is still a long way to go in departments before members are afforded appropriate support. That is the only way suicide and alcoholism will be less of a risk.

This was also a turning point for me—I considered leaving policing. But then I realized a narcotics officer was not in high demand anywhere else and that my Grade 13 education would not carry me far, so I made a conscious decision to attend university part-time; reduce my amortization on my mortgage (with the goal of being mortgage free by the time I reached twenty years' service); and put myself in a position to remain in the force only for as long as it worked for me and my family. You may ask why I would consider leaving the force, something I had worked so hard to get in to and even harder to establish a positive reputation within. Simply put, the impact this event had on my wife was profound, and as we were considering starting a family, I was unsure I wanted to introduce my future children to this environment.

If it hadn't been for Rod Stamler and Dick Dickens, I would have likely followed through with leaving. Rod gave me considerable leeway to foster new programs and take on responsibilities often assigned to higher ranks. Additionally, he assigned me to university training after I showed interest through enrolling in night courses. This support renewed my faith in the force and enabled me to bury the year and a half of living under threat. When we were finally permitted to return to our home in North Gower, the house was alarmed, there were bars on the windows, and there was a direct link to the VIP Protection Detail unit, which coordinated with the OPP, who were the police of jurisdiction.

Over that year and a half, whenever the alarm went off, there'd be an OPP and an RCMP response, all of whom arrived with guns drawn. The RCMP embassy patrol also had our home on their patrol route, so they would pass by our house five or six times per day. As you can imagine, living in a relatively rural area, we became the talk of the neighbourhood. Initially, some were concerned about what we might be bringing to the area, while others thought the extra policing patrols were extremely beneficial. On top of this, the RCMP provided us with a German shepherd for added protection and peace of mind. The shepherd listened to me but defied my wife whenever I was travelling back to BC for court. Sadly, our neighbour's son, while waiting for the school bus, would throw stones at him. The dog was in a kennel, but we knew if he broke out, the youth would be toast, so we had to give the dog to a shelter. Although these provisions did afford some peace of mind, I still travelled back and forth to the office alone, and other than my revolver, this was the extent of my security. I did feel that my threat was being resolved the more I got through my testimony—the reality is, once I'd testified in the preliminary hearing, that evidence could be brought into trial, and at that stage, killing me would not have negated any of the charges against the accused individuals—but the ongoing security, tripping of alarms, and armed police response does start to weigh on a family.

Chapter Thirteen

THE REALITY OF HQ SETS IN

Working in HQ was both eye-opening and frustrating. After a few weeks, Dick Dickens advised me to write down everything I hated about HQ and to seek a transfer the day I started changing my tune, as that's when I would know that I had become indoctrinated into HQ's status-seeking culture. This was sound advice.

Commissioner Robert Henry Simmonds was at the helm of the RCMP when I arrived in Ottawa and he remained so until 1987. My observation was that he was the old-school paramilitary type but had a deep respect for the working officers. I am not sure that was the case for the commissioned-officer cadre who often felt the wrath of his displeasure. Uniquely, I was the only constable in HQ at the time, which gave me some status within the ranks. Being a constable who'd just completed a high-level undercover operation earned me some notoriety, along with the respect of the commissioner.

Rod Stamler, the OIC of the drug branch and an officer I admired and respected, continually told me to be true to myself and to stay in the force as long as I was happy and able to contribute, and if possible, to leave on a high note. This advice guided me later in my career when I left the force.

Rod was, in my view, an officer ahead of his time. He was willing to think outside the box and never let rank get in the way of moving programs along. Rod was also able to identify and weigh an individual's unique capabilities and used that discernment to add value to the drug enforcement program, though it often resulted in a lower-ranked member undertaking an assignment normally reserved for more senior ranks. I admired this trait of his immensely, and his management style worked well with my personality and drive.

Unfortunately, Rod was singular in this approach—most of the management above him relied on old-fashioned paramilitary practices and prioritized seniority over ability when it came time to offer promotions. Over and over again, senior leaders played politics rather than take a stand on policing issues, if it looked like those concerns may lead to opposition from politicians.

I recognize that many police leaders will disagree with me on this point, but I would argue that unless police leaders are prepared to be candid with our political masters and push back when politics impacts the safety and security of Canada, we will fail miserably. This has been proven time and time again. China is a case in point (one I will focus on later), but suffice to say our political masters have sacrificed security for potential economic foreign relationships leading to increased trade. Meanwhile, our police leaders remain silent on the issue.

Due to fact that the RCMP is federal and therefore has to answer to Parliament, it has, for the most part, had a centralized reporting structure in that certain operational requirements (e.g., international travel, flash rolls of significant size, various undercover requests) require HQ's approval. HQ was an interesting environment. Most Fridays we would go out for lunch, often with Drug Enforcement Administration (DEA) attaché Len Ripzinsky. We would seldom return for the day. In most cases, the group included the majority of the drug enforcement branch, so we would often use telecoms to check if any urgent requests were waiting.

On one occasion, an urgent request arrived from Vancouver Drugs while we were all enjoying a largely liquid lunch. As I was a junior person, it was on me to return to the office to seek the authority of Assistant Commissioner Randy Schramm, a very old-school officer. Fortunately for me, I had garnered a fair degree of respect from Randy based on my prior case analysis and recommendations, so when I went to his office with a recommendation, I simply said, "Please don't ask, it's all good, and I want to reply to Vancouver." This could have gone either way—Randy could have severely reprimanded not only me but my bosses—but luckily Randy let me make the call and we never heard any more from him, much to the relief of several inspectors.

A few early assignments that Rod had given me involved meeting with Admiral Daniel J. Murphy in Washington, DC, and acting as the force's representative, despite the fact that I was only a corporal. I was to ascertain US expectations for the RCMP role. The initiative was termed the National Narcotics Border Interdiction System and was supported by then vice president George Bush Sr. When we met in Washington, Admiral Murphy could not have been a more gracious host. Going into the meeting, I was accompanied by Inspector Ralph DeGroot, who was the RCMP representative in Washington. Admiral Murphy was being attended to by a number of representatives from various organizations in the room. He immediately asked everyone to leave except me and we had a frank conversation in which I emphasized I would be acting as a messenger only.

Some time after my stints in Washington, Rod Stamler, with the agreement of Deputy Henry Jensen, created a temporary post in Florida due to the number of drugs coming into Canada from South Florida. I was assigned to oversee this post. It became abundantly obvious that Commissioner Simmonds had not been briefed on this, resulting in his requesting the file at a time when both Rod and Deputy Jensen were travelling. A handwritten note from Simmonds came back to Inspector Don Willett with a series of questions, the majority of which asked *Who's Garry?*—Simmonds claimed he did not recall commissioning anyone by that name. This inquiry stemmed from the fact that when Rod and I wrote back and forth we used first names, which is not the paramilitary way. When Willett received this letter, he told me this would not go well—it was bad that the commissioner hadn't been briefed about the Miami position. When he showed me the commissioner's note, I wanted to go up to Simmonds's office, seeing as he wanted to know who I was, but this did not happen until Rod returned.

We ended up in a meeting with Stamler, Dickens, and the commissioner, who asked me, "Corp, what would you do if you were being misled?" I realized this was a no-win situation for me regardless of my answer—if I supported my bosses, I'd be going against the commissioner; if I agreed with the commissioner, I'd be distancing myself from my bosses—so I simply replied that this was why he was the commissioner. I was dismissed from the meeting.

Commissioner Simmonds did not suffer fools and was a staunch believer in the chain of command.

Also during this time, I was asked to put together a novel conference for Jensen, which we were calling the Franco-American-Italian-Canadian Drug and Organized-Crime Conference. I commandeered my colleague Kim Marsh, and the two of us set out to make all the arrangements for the event. During the conference, we had the opportunity to meet Judge Falcone. Giovanni Falcone was an Italian judge and prosecuting magistrate. He spoke about the Sicilian Mafia and how Italian law enforcement were in the process of launching a large investigation aimed at reducing the Mafia's power. Along with DEA Director Francis M. "Bud" Mullen, all participants offered full support to Judge Falcone, considering how the Mafia had spread out in various countries. Judge Falcone was extremely gracious and tremendously interesting as he articulated the struggles Italy faced. Tragically, he was executed May 23, 1992, after spearheading the Maxi Trial in 1986 and 1987.

It was around this time that I also reached out to Brent Crowhurst in Halifax to discuss establishing a ship-boarding course, seeing as we were dealing with an increase in large ships transporting drugs. With Brent's contacts, the RCMP created the first ship-boarding course in Canada. The reality was that the boats we had available to us on the East Coast were far too small to be taken seriously. Working with what we had, we collaborated with the Coast Guard and with Fisheries and Oceans Canada to practice boarding large vessels. I am sure my fingerprints are still embedded in the rope ladder we used to climb from our small vessel onto the Fisheries vessel.

In the evenings, seeing as we had a few musically talented members who played for Newfie Bullet, we went around to the local pubs. Our talent was well received. A couple days before finishing the course, we presented the commander of the Mill Cove telecommunications military base with an RCMP ball cap. At some point in the evening it went missing, so the base commander locked down the base until it was returned by one of his personnel. This two-week training event became known around Headquarters as the greatest scam organized at that period—many of my colleagues couldn't believe I'd gotten away with getting a two-week vacation under the guise of badly needed training—but it was a great two weeks and we learned a lot, mainly that our small-craft vessels were totally inadequate to take on "mothership" loads of drugs.

During this period, I began to realize the RCMP needed to refocus and apply stricter guidelines to the duration of time members spent in Headquarters. As I was becoming more comfortable "speaking truth to power," especially with Rod Stamler, I wrote a paper recommending that Headquarters become a limited-duration posting, thereby providing exposure to more members and ensuring members stay current with the realities in the field. I worked with individuals who had spent the majority of their career in Headquarters, and I formed the view that they would be better described as civil servants than as police officers. Uniform officers riding public transit without being in possession of a firearm just never sat right with me. Society expects police officers in uniform to be able to provide assistance regardless of the seriousness of the issue. Requiring an officer to publicly wear a uniform with no weapon, especially following 9/11, is careless and puts both officers and civilians riding transit at risk. Later, I witnessed members come in as sergeants and make their way up the ranks all the way to deputy commissioner without ever returning to operations. (Currently there are only five deputy commissioners in the RCMP: one for contract and Indigenous policing; one for federal policing; one for special services; one for British Columbia; and one for Alberta.) This resulted in those members' total lack of appreciation for court decisions like Jordan and Stinchcombe and how these cases can complicate criminal investigations. These cases, which, in service of a speedy trial, mandate full and timely disclosure of an entire investigation, create tremendous challenges. Unless you've experienced the reality of working in an operational undercover unit, you cannot really comprehend the negative impact of such decisions on our investigations. Seeing as many commissioned officers fell into this category, ignorant of what complex investigations involve at the operational level, it is no wonder our politicians never received appropriate briefings on how their decisions were affecting our investigative capacity in Canada to tackle organized crime, money laundering, and transnational criminal activities. In my view, this was the beginning of the end of the force's ability to be seen as a leader—from this point on, following the Supreme Court's Jordan decision in 2016, investigations that normally would've been carried out by a team of four to five investigators now require twenty-plus investigators, inclusive of legal assistance, major-case managers, accountants, and managers of seized property. With so few seasoned managers at the "officer" level, investigations have not been prioritized as they should have.

Chapter Fourteen

ANTI-DRUG PROFITEERING

While all of the events in the last chapter were occurring, I was fortunate to be able to commence studies at the University of Ottawa. I focused my studies on business, as this background would allow me to be assigned to the Anti–Drug Profiteering program, the embryonic precursor to today's Proceeds of Crime program. Initially I worked with Wayne Blackburn, but following his promotion to training I was placed in charge in an acting sergeant role. Rod Stamler's support was impeccable; he gave me the latitude to build out a program, including training for investigators and non-commissioned officers. Additionally, I was afforded the opportunity to speak internationally.

This opportunity paved the way for the direction of the remainder of my career. I had embraced the fact that simply arresting large-scale criminals, seizing their drugs, and prosecuting them solved nothing. Based on what I'd witnessed in my undercover assignments, it was evident that we needed to go after the money.

At this time, Commissioner Norman Inkster took command. It was evident that Henry Jensen was hoping to be appointed, but his aspirations came to an abrupt end on March 12, 1985.

This was the date when agents of the Armenian Revolutionary Army attacked the Turkish embassy in Ottawa. Inside the embassy, the assailants rounded up at least twelve hostages, including the wife of the Turkish ambassador, his teenage daughter, and embassy staff members. The attack resulted in a single death, the on-duty security officer Claude Brunelle—a thirty-year-old student at the University of Ottawa—who shot at the gunmen and was shot in return, and killed instantly.[7] The attack on the Turkish embassy was a major international embarrassment for Canada. For years, foreign diplomats in Ottawa had asked the Canadian government for better security, but to no avail.[8] Turkey declared Ottawa to be one of the most dangerous places in the world for Turkish diplomats. Canada needed a unit that was capable of defeating a determined and well-armed group of militants. But this need was ignored until the attack. This event changed the Canadian government's attitude toward militants and led to the creation of the RCMP's Special Emergency Response Team.[9]

As is always the way in Ottawa, someone had to be blamed for the failure; that blame fell on Deputy Jensen, which thwarted any chance of his becoming commissioner.

Around this same time, I wrote the LSATs and was accepted into the University of Ottawa Faculty of Law. I requested that the force consider sponsoring me so that I could attend. Stamler supported me, as did Jensen, who forwarded my correspondence to Deputy Commissioner Inkster. I received correspondence back from his office that as I did not have a full degree, I did not meet the criteria for sponsorship. Unbeknownst to Inkster, I had spoken to Inspector Frank Palmer, a member who had acquired a law degree through the force as a mature student with no prior full degree. Knowing this, I wrote back through the chain of command. In hindsight, I likely used the wrong word—I stated that I was "perplexed" by the decision, seeing as it was not in keeping with past practices.

The curt reply that came back clearly showed that the deputy did not like to be challenged or proven incorrect.

Commissioner Simmonds was looking to retire, and both Inkster and Jensen were in the running for his position. I am not sure that Jensen's overwhelming support of my schooling was appreciated by the soon-to-be Commissioner Inkster. My request was denied. What bothered me most was not the denial, but the fact that senior management strayed from past practice and then held that policy did not permit a person without a full degree to go to law school, when this was clearly not the case.

In my role as acting sergeant with the Anti–Drug Profiteering program, I was fortunate to traverse the country to provide training in concert with Sergeant Bob Preston from Edmonton. Together we trained many of the various police services, highlighting the value of looking at the finances of criminal organizations along with their predicate offences. In my view, Bob Preston was the most motivated and forward-thinking investigator in the program at this time. Through his efforts, we were able to demonstrate to the government the value of attacking the proceeds of crime to call attention to the sore spots that were present in Canadian legislation.

Rod had also enabled me to be somewhat operational and to support the newly formed Anti–Drug Profiteering units, thereby permitting me to keep my foot in operations. I was able to work on a number of files, including the Cuntrera-Caruana Montreal file. Italian prosecutors described the Cuntrera-Caruana Mafia clan as an "international holding ... a holding which secures certain services for the Sicilian Cosa Nostra as a whole: drug-trafficking routes and channels for money laundering."The clan is "a very tight-knit family group of 'men of honour,' not only joined by Mafia bonds, but also by ties of blood." According to the Italian Antimafia Commission, the Cuntrera-Caruana clan played a central role in international drug trafficking, extending their interests from Italy to Canada and Ve nezuela.[10] My assistance included an analysis of the money flows and evidence gathered in the UK, where heroin was secreted away in furniture. A total of $36,217,918 had been deposited in various institutions from 1978 to 1984, including six hundred thousand dollars in cash to institutions in Switzerland.

A second investigation, dubbed Project Highway, involved Raynald Desjardins, a prominent organized-crime figure in Montreal and an associate of the Rizzuto crime family. In this investigation we witnessed a financial flow from Montreal to London to Cyprus, and then on to Lebanon. A drug shipment was then taken onto a large ship and was off-loaded on Canada's east coast. A financial analysis showed that there were 22,636 kilos of marijuana with a value of $3,250 per kilo, for a potential revenue of $73,568,300—almost seventy-five million dollars. I was directly involved in preparing the analysis, which showed that 15,818 kilos had been seized, and that the purchase price of the drugs overseas was $280 per kilo. Considering shipping costs and equipment, the profit would be $14,615,473, nearly fifteen million dollars. This is why drug trafficking is so pervasive—because it's enormously lucrative. This case also showed how Canadian banks at that time failed to conduct due diligence on deposits, and how much real estate and luxury items were valued by the criminal organization.

A file that caught my attention was one Bob Preston had taken on in Edmonton, wherein an individual named Stephen Pakozdy and his wife were laundering money through a furniture-store front. The investigation commenced after the seizure of $486,500 at the airport from Pakozdy. This was the first case in which I put together an expert affidavit to assist the judge to help them understand money laundering and to show just how Pakozdy had obtained an unidentified income of about five hundred thousand dollars. I was in Edmonton with Bob and the federal prosecutor for the Department of Justice (DOJ) accessing the full file, which included photographs, in order to assist the case. I'd like to remind you that at this time, most files were not digitized, and we sometimes had to travel to access paper files and meet with investigators and DOJ lawyers. I am sure I looked like a deer in headlights when I realized that Pakozdy's wife was a girl I had dated for a short time in Elmira. When I asked if she was from Elmira, the look on Bob's and the prosecutor's faces were interesting, to say the least. Certainly proved we live in a small world.

After speaking to a group from the UN in Spain as well as to New Scotland Yard and Her Majesty's Customs and Excise, I was invited to be the keynote speaker at the annual conference hosted by the International Association of Chiefs of Police in England. This invitation was supported, again, by Rod and Deputy Jensen, but seeing as it was international, it required Commissioner Inkster's approval. The commissioner sat on the approval until two days before I was scheduled to travel. Then, he walked the approval down to our offices, stepped in, and tossed the approval at me, saying, "You can go," and left.

I know many people would have done nothing. Many people would've just accepted this approval as a plus, regardless of the attitude with which it was given, but that wasn't in my psyche. I took the approval and walked back up to Inkster's office. I told him that as my wife had just given birth to our second child, I really didn't care whether I went to England or not, but that I felt this was a good opportunity for the force. I will give the commissioner full marks, as he did apologize, saying he was not happy with the processes being applied by my bosses. I am sure, however, that he did not readily forgive me for this interaction.

It was truly interesting to witness how politics played such a destructive role within the force at this time. Rod Stamler had become the face and voice for the RCMP due to his proactivity in the drug-and-money-laundering arena. He was invited around the world to speak on his approaches, and he definitely upstaged the commissioner. In fact, one invitation incorrectly referred to him as commissioner. It became evident that this was a sore spot for

Commissioner Inkster, which ultimately led to Rod's transfer out of the drug branch.

The media repeatedly reports that senior RCMP leadership has failed on many levels. This failure in management is due to a lack of understanding of how power and politics are utilized in the day-to-day operations of a large organization. During this period of my career, I undertook studies for a fourth-year course required to obtain a Bachelor of Commerce. When I think back on the results—the value that higher education added to my work, including the credibility I earned among some senior managers and the upgrade in my qualifications for financial investigations—it helps me understand what occurred during this period of my career and through to the present day.

The University of Ottawa course I took in 1985 was under the direct supervision of Dr. Swee Goh. I did not have to attend class, but I had to, much like a regular graduate student, select a topic and prepare a paper under the guidance of the professor. The topic I selected was "power in politics," and the requirement was to delve into how senior management within the RCMP were able to handle the political ramifications of working in proximity to the government while managing their teams effectively. We used a verified questionnaire, previously utilized by a Harvard University professor, and sent it out to senior RCMP management.

One interesting finding, which remains current in today's policing environment, was that senior management espouses the view that the force's reputation speaks for itself, and that it is not a police function to debate established policies or practices with the public. The overall conclusion from the study was that RCMP senior managers are extremely inept when it comes to understanding power and politics conceptually.

If we look at recent events and today's reality, I would submit that we are witnessing real-life examples of what that study brought to light. Sadly, the study was dismissed outright. But perhaps what we witness in policing today *does* speak for itself.

I spent over three years in an acting sergeant role in Anti–Drug Profiteering before the position went to staffing for permanency. Assistant Commissioner Rod Stamler assured me that I would be considered the front runner for the permanent position. Unfortunately, promotions were not based on background but seniority. Notwithstanding the fact that many senior officers across Canada wrote to Stamler supporting the value I provided to them and the program, Deputy Commissioner John Moffat, an old-school manager, ruled that another member with no experience in the Proceeds of Crime program (but senior to me) was to be selected. Rod had gone to great lengths for me and was as disappointed as I was, so when he offered me a chance to go on to French-language training, I jumped at it.

I spent fourteen months on French-language training. During that period, Rod was transferred, which in my view was clearly a political move due to his increasingly public persona in becoming the face of the RCMP. Rod's replacement did not even realize I was part of his unit. Of course, when he found out, I was directed to return to the office and it became evident I would not last long in the unit.

Remember Dick Dicken's advice when I started at HQ? To detail all the things I disliked about it and then, when I started looking at the list wanting to change what I initially thought, to know that it would be time to transfer out? Well, my list had come home to roost. I realized I needed to go back to some form of operational policing.

Chapter Fifteen

PARLIAMENT HILL BUS HIJACKING

On April 7, 1989, a Greyhound bus was hijacked in Montreal and driven to Parliament Hill, where the bus got stuck on the front lawn of the Centre Block.[11] Having taken a newly devised advanced hostage-negotiation course, I was asked to assist, along with Brian Sargent and Inspector Alain Théoret of the Ottawa Police Service. As I had just completed French-language training, this was a real test—the negotiation was conducted in French. The hijacker, Charles Yacoub, thought I was a psychologist, so evidently we developed a rapport. After several hours, I was able to convince Yacoub to surrender and release the hostages.

The stress I experienced was worse than it had been with the alleged contract; I knew that one mistake could result in triggering the hijacker and in him killing the hostages. On top of this, French was not my strong suit, so it required my full mental ability to keep the discussion flowing.

Sergeant-at-Arms Major-General Gus Cloutier commended our team following the successful conclusion and assured us we would get recognition. Well, allow me to describe the recognition. A few days following this event, I spoke to a doctor, as the stress was seriously affecting me. Again, no programs to assist. A week later, I was told I was under investigation because of a complaint that I spoke English initially and had had the bus driver translate to Yacoub.

I was not seeking recognition for doing my job, but this investigation was a slap in the face. It was allowed to unfold because senior managers were playing politics and did not understanding how negotiation works. To me, this showed just how political the force was becoming.

Not long after this, I was invited to speak to the Advocates' Society in Toronto about negotiating under duress. In my address, I argued that my undercover experience was the best training for negotiation, since high-level traffickers and organized-crime criminals are extremely effective negotiators—they're acutely aware that offending someone can result in dire consequences.

I also pointed out that the officers on-site that day were more concerned about being in a command centre then commencing the negotiation, and that those overseeing the operation had little, if any, experience on what it takes to negotiate a win-win scenario. One example I used as a lose-lose situation was the Meech Lake Accord, which was a failed attempt to add Quebec's consent to the Constitution under the tenure of Brian Mulroney. Hosted by the prime minister, this meeting of the provinces failed through negotiation to obtain the agreement of Quebec. Although politics can be a hard showstopper, the reality is that everyone needs to come to the table with a win-win approach. I concluded my address with the following statement: "In conclusion, we negotiate every day of our lives. It takes only courage to be successful, as with courage one soon adopts a strategy of being a 'win-winner,' the only strategy that will instill a sense of accomplishment."

After being passed over for the Anti–Drug Profiteering promotion, I opted to take a transfer to embassy patrol, where as a sergeant, I would be supervising a large team, as I was aspiring to become a commissioned officer. My decision to transfer was also influenced by the fact that Assistant Commissioner Marcel Coutu had launched a character assassination of me after I stood up to Sergeant Bruce Bowie, the individual who won the the Anti-Drug Profiteering promotion due to seniority. I stood up to him because he had overindulged the previous night and was not fit for purpose the next day when he attempted to deliver training. This resulted in the officers in attendance at Peel Regional Police initially wanting to scrap the rest of the training; however, with some coaxing, the rest of the provided training was well received. The Peel Regional investigators stepped in, and I also ended up providing a full day of training, which was well received and ultimately redeemed us. Suffice to say, it smoothed my ruffled feathers, as there ended up being some positive value in the day.

Well, Marcel wrote a scathing dissertation on my evaluation. I vehemently objected to it. We went toe to toe for over an hour, and I continually threatened to refer the matter to Deputy Commissioner Jensen. Marcel finally agreed to withdraw his comments about my conduct and permitted me to transfer to embassy patrol.

I tolerated ten months in the protective policing arena, which, although important, was work I viewed as akin to that of a glorified security guard, which was the furthest thing from how I was used to operating. Protective policing serves an important function but requires a different mindset from investigative policing. I witnessed how the prime minister's residence was protected by officers whose skills were (in my view) sub-standard. I joked that we seemed to put the members who were least comfortable patrolling at the most prestigious locations. This was at a time when we had engaged special constables, some of whom were former military and very competent, while others who had been hired quickly following the incident at the Turkish embassy had not been subject to rigorous standards in the process, resulting in some serious inconsistencies in the talent—some patrollers who excelled at their job and others who performed extremely poorly.

So, I lobbied for a transfer to HQ's foreign services, where I was assigned the Western Hemisphere, which meant coordinating with our liaison officers in this area. During this tenure I was asked to do a desk audit of our Hong Kong post. To ensure an unbiased approach, I sought input from the divisions across Canada, the OPP, and the Toronto Police Service. The findings were disappointing.

My desk audit proved anything but flattering. History showed it was a predominantly administrative post whose main role was socializing with senior police officials, all of whom were listed in the report, citing concrete examples. Operational requests were either ignored or responded to in a manner to add no value to investigations; this was to the point that the Toronto Police Service had quit sending requests, and the Vancouver RCMP would rely only on direct Royal Hong Kong Police contact to ensure they got assistance—which was against policy. At this time, I had completed my commission-officer process, which meant I would be put on a list for promotion. The officer in charge, Luc Generoux, recommended I take a posting to Hong Kong with the aim of operationalizing the post. By that I mean connecting force-wide with investigative sections and with our policing partners to obtain access to any of their files involving Hong Kong, while also responding quickly to inquiries from Canada. I agreed, with the proviso that I would replace the OIC upon his retirement. Luc assured me that this would be the case, that he had conferred with Inkster, and they would pass his title to me when George Gibbs retired from Hong Kong in a year.

Given what Luc had imparted to me, I ensured that Canada's consulate general in Hong Kong was made aware that I was to become the head of the RCMP liaison office after a year. All of this was set in writing with Luc's full knowledge and, to my understanding, sent to the commissioner.

In 1991, just prior to leaving for Hong Kong, I received word from a civilian member that they heard another inspector would be going. I broached this immediately with Luc and he assured me this would not happen. I asked him to get assurances from Commissioner Inkster and was told he did.

Additionally at this time, I was approached by staffing, who inquired whether I wished to go to law school. Realize, my transfer was already out for Hong Kong, I had leased my house, and had planned for my furniture's storage. Although law school had been a long-sought-after desire, the query made no sense, and the timing could not have come at a worse time. The left hand really did not know what the right was doing.

Part Five

MID-CAREER

Chapter Sixteen

ASIAN-BASED ORGANIZED CRIME

Upon my arrival in Hong Kong, I learned that my unflattering review of the Hong Kong office had been provided to their inspector. This immediately put us at odds. Then, six weeks into the posting, I heard officially that the inspector rumoured to be transferred to Hong Kong rather than me would be coming after all. I wrote a scathing email to Luc for his bold-faced lie. Fortunately, Superintendent Claude Sweeney and Staff Sergeant Bob Ramsay were both aware of Luc's promise, but Inkster was steadfast in his decision. He stood by Gary Lagimodiere being George's replacement. Regardless of all this, I put my head down and decided I would do my minimum three years as staff sergeant under Lagimodiere and ensure the post was operational. This news did not sit well with my wife and family, who reluctantly came with me, and truly soured my wife on the honesty of senior force management.

This posting afforded me the opportunity to become educated in the organized-crime group known as "the triads." The best analogy I can use to explain triads is that they are the Chinese equivalent of North America's outlaw motorcycle gang, the Hells Angels. Triads are a Chinese transnational organized-crime syndicate who have established themselves throughout the world using the Chinese diaspora. I worked closely with the Organized Crime and Triad Bureau (a division of the Hong Kong Police) and quickly gained the trust of the operational officers, as they viewed me as someone who was finally interested in police operations. Rather than socializing with the upper echelons and going out in the evenings to the local police haunts for dinner and beers, I chose to socialize with the working officers who oversaw operations. Officers who were boots on the ground. This period of my career allowed me to gain an understanding of Asian-based organized crime in Canada and its relationship with China.

Shortly after arriving in Hong Kong, I was invited to the China Building, where I was introduced to a number of senior Chinese officials. Being the consummate diplomat that I am, I had a conversation with a general in which we discussed the Tiananmen Square massacre, which had occurred two years before my arrival. He asked me what Canada would do if a hundred thousand people with the IQ of a monkey stormed the city, causing problems. He then stated that we treat our "Indian" population the same as they treated their student demonstrators. I will never forget that response.

At this time (pre-1997, before Hong Kong reverted back to China), there was a high demand for immigration to Canada. Unfortunately, being a member of a triad society did not constitute grounds to prohibit entry to Canada, since we did not have a similar criminal offence here in our country. The entrepreneur program required a certain level of wealth, and triads and triad-affiliated individuals easily met the required threshold. One immigration officer who worked diligently to thwart their applications was Brian McAdam. Unfortunately, Brian's views often went unacknowledged. He quickly brought me up to speed, and together we wrote countless briefs on various applicants, relying heavily on intelligence provided from the Royal Hong Kong Police (RHKP). Additionally, we wrote a manuscript on triads that was widely distributed and sanctioned by the RHKP.

Our many briefs, which were forwarded to the RCMP Headquarters, later became the catalyst for an intelligence probe entitled "Operation Sidewinder" (which I will discuss further in the book). The deluge of intelligence afforded us by the RHKP was impressive. It should have been a wake-up call to the Canadian government and its senior intelligence officials.

In September 1992, knowing amendments were underway in Canada for immigration, and hearing that no consideration had been given to codifying that being a member of (or affiliated with) an organized-crime group would prohibit entry into Canada, I did an interview with Ben Tierney of Southam News and explained the full extent of what was occurring. I knew this could cost me my job, but there comes a point in life when it is more important to do the right thing, and in a timely manner. Many will argue that I was wrong to do the interview, but happily, it had the desired effect: legislation was passed.

Ironically, some in Ottawa believed that the section would not pass a Charter challenge and that the enactment was politically motivated. What no one anticipated was that upon my return, I would be engaged to provide expert evidence in the first test case wherein the new legislation was challenged. The Honourable Austin F. Cullen, the sitting federal-court justice, heard the evidence in camera. The DOJ lawyer stated, "Inspector Clement's viva voce evidence went over extremely well and the judge was clearly impressed with the expert evidence that Inspector Clement gave in this matter." While I'd taken a risk to get the message out publicly, the outcome was extremely beneficial to Canada.

As the liaison officer in Asia, my territory included Japan, South Korea, Taiwan, China, and the Philippines. We learned that each of these jurisdictions had their share of organized crime. Japan is notorious for the Yamaguchi family (also known as the yakuza) and the *bōryokudan* ("violence groups"); these are well-known transnational organized-crime groups that have a three-hundred-year history.

The Philippines' biggest export is women; sadly, the country has been a supplier to organized-crime groups for human trafficking. I had opportunities to meet with Philippine law enforcement and unfortunately, the export of women is widely accepted, with the belief that the majority are household workers who allow for a flow of money back to the women's families. In reality, many of the young girls are employed in the sex trade under the control of organized crime.

Many of the women working the Macau casinos were Filipina, Malaysian, or Eastern European. All of these women were under direct control of the triads. There was a strong indication that exchanges occurred amongst various organized-crime groups. In other words, women were a commodity to be sold and traded. One case I worked on involved women being exported to Canada. During this period, women were permitted to get a work visa to Canada under the auspices of an exotic-dancer exchange provision. When I delved into this, I was able to uncover that two locations in Canada worked with triad groups to get women into their places of business. The most disheartening part of this immigration regulation was that it was supported by Barbara McDougall, who was then the minister of employment and immigration.

I remember an instance when a well-known immigration lawyer wrote the head of the immigration department in Hong Kong, expressing concern for the holdup on the working visas for a group of women, arguing that they were a benefit to Canada and helped to ensure marriages survived. You can't make this shit up.

One case that highlights how valuable a liaison officer is to Canadian law enforcement involved the kidnapping of a Taiwanese citizen who was attending university in BC. The Vancouver Police sought our assistance when it was ascertained that the father, a Taiwanese surgeon, had been contacted and directed to pay a ransom in Hong Kong. This immediately brought in the need for the full cooperation of the Hong Kong Police Force, who sought to have a Canadian representative present. Although we received pushback by the OIC, I agreed to be in the ops centre of the Hong Kong Police and coordinate with Vancouver. Fortunately, the case unfolded as it should; the kidnapping victim was returned, the perpetrators and ransom were located in Hong Kong, and the perpetrators in Vancouver arrested.

Superintendent Sweeney had backed up my position to get involved in the case, despite the OIC's disagreement. The previous practice that liaison officers were not allowed to engage in active investigations was based on the view that they might become a compellable witness back in Canada. Meanwhile, our counterparts in the United States and Australia took the opposite approach— their liaison officers worked closely with local law enforcement in an effort to ensure criminal cases were successfully investigated. The position adopted by the OIC was based on his training, but I took the strong view that his opinion was out of date and served little to no overall benefit for Canada. His statement that we liaison officers were nothing more than a glorified mail drop was flawed and served no useful purpose.

It was disturbing to me that Canadians assigned to the high commission saw nothing wrong with receiving free trips to the jockey club, including receiving *lai see* packets (red envelopes) and money for gambling. This, along with frequent junkets offered by various high–net worth individuals, raised many alarm bells for me, as it was, in my view, the endorsement of corrupt practices. The high commissioner welcomed individuals like Stanley Ho and Cheng Yu-tung, who had many connections to triads. The former premier of BC was even photographed with the father of the head of the Sun Yee On triad society, which was published in the *South China Morning Post*. On one occasion, through a trusted Hong Kong friend, I was offered an opportunity to meet Stanley Ho and have a discussion on "triads." When the high commissioner got wind of this, he, along with the officer in charge, forbade me from taking the meeting, despite the fact that Ho was applying for Canadian status.

In the early nineties, I learned that the high commissioner and his family had spent time with a known 426 "Red Pole" triad office bearer in Toronto while on holidays. I confronted the high commissioner and advised him he likely would have shown up on any potential surveillance that may have been undertaken. He claimed he had no knowledge of the individual being a 14K Triad member and office bearer and was very surprised, which seemed to be a theme for many politicians and high-commission staff.

Around that same time, I also had the opportunity to attend the "Asian Crime Conference" in Las Vegas. Two officers from HQ also were in attendance: George Allen and Claude Savoie. I had gotten to know both these officers during my time in HQ and through interactions with Divisions. Claude was known to have worked organized crime in Montreal and always appeared from the outside to have a strong commitment to taking whatever enforcement action was available. On December 22, 1992, Claude died by suicide in his office in HQ. It was revealed that he was under investigation for leaking information to Allan "the Weasel" Ross of the West End Gang during Claude's time in the drug section in Montreal. His boss was Bryan McConnell, who later became my commanding officer in the National Capital Region. Savoie shot himself the day before the CBC current-affairs show *The Fifth Estate* was set to air a segment on Ross and the West End Gang. It was a widely held belief that Ross was never prosecuted in Canada because he had high-placed informants within Canadian police departments. *The Fifth Estate* reported private meetings between Ross and Savoie at a downtown restaurant and in the offices of Ross's lawyer, Sidney Leithman, who was murdered in 1990.[12]

For someone who has worked in organized crime and survived death threats, having someone you had judged as solid investigator against organized crime surface as a traitor shocks your basic foundational beliefs and leaves a feeling of total betrayal. You start reflecting on what you'd discussed with that person, and how that person could be so callous. This renewed my view that anyone can be co-opted. It also renewed my resolve to ensure any information involving corruption would be investigated in a timely and effective manner.

This incident followed on the heels of another case in which I recommended a highly respected financial-crime investigator for a position at the United Nations; it was later revealed that he had retrieved a financial seizure from Vancouver Police and failed to return the money as an RCMP exhibit. A few years later, on March 10, 1996, Larry Silzer, a former staff sergeant in Vancouver's RCMP and a world authority on money laundering, was convicted of fraud (though he did repay the money he stole).

During that conference in Las Vegas, Superintendent Claude Savoie, another officer from HQ, and I held a meeting with the FBI focused on the impact of triads in North America. The FBI took the position that this was a non-issue—they did not have a triad problem. I responded that this was a fair statement if one never looked, but I vehemently communicated that statements like theirs create bigger problems, ones that come back to bite us in the future.

Also in 1992, I met with investigative journalist Terry Gould through Jerry Moloci of Vancouver Drugs. Gould had been early and influential in his reporting on the activities of triad member Steven Wong, who was alleged to have fled to Macau after being charged and of then feigning his death. When Gould arrived in my office, I initially thought he had a death wish, as he wanted to go to Macau and, after establishing sufficient proof he may still be alive, track down Wong in a community controlled by the 14K Triads, and arrange to have him arrested with an extradition request made from Canada.

In order to assist, I reached out to Tony Salvado, a Macau officer for whom I had the utmost respect. We had met on numerous occasions and I felt he could be trusted; he was a solid and credible officer. He had explained to me that he'd been offered a promotion to go to traffic (you could make a fortune keeping fines for traffic violations), but Tony refused to be co-opted because it would mean being in the pockets of some of his less-than-honest superiors as well as some notorious triad figures.

Gould *did* travel to Macau and allegedly spotted Wong getting on the hydrofoil that travelled between Hong Kong and Macau. Unfortunately, at this time I was also working an international drug case involving the US, Hong Kong, and Canada, which would lead to the arrest of Kong Kim-fai. Kong was arrested for heroin importation to Canada and was a subject of high interest to the American authorities. Intelligence indicated he was a top man in a Hong Kong syndicate believed to have been trafficking drugs for ten years from the Far East to Australia, Europe, and North America. It was further alleged that he had been behind recent imports into Canada responsible for the deaths of seventy drug users due to the heroin's purity. Kong was arrested by Senior Inspector Pat Laidler of the Wan Chai office of the Narcotics Bureau along with a co-conspirator, Chu King-shing.

Extradition was requested by the DOJ so that both could appear in Vancouver to answer to charges. On September 17, 1993, the *South China Morning Post* reported the following:

> Senior Crown Counsel Roger McMeans told the court the Hong Kong government had received a request from the Canadian authorities for Chu and Kong's arrests and extraditions. McMeans said the investigation into the syndicate began following Canada customs' interception of eight large framed pictures containing about seven kilograms of No. 4 heroin sent via airmail from Bangkok to Vancouver.[13]

McMeans told the magistrate that Kong had allegedly paid an individual eighty thousand dollars to go to Canada to accept delivery of the pictures, with heroin concealed in their frames.

Investigations led to Hong Kong where Kong and Chu were picked up for questioning and arrested. Kong, who had seven previous convictions (but none for drug trafficking) sought bail on grounds that he had three children and aging parents to support. Bail was denied and Kong was to be brought back to court in September 1993, when it was expected he would announce if he intended to fight his extradition.

Due to my involvement in the Kong case, I was not available to respond to Gould on the spur of the moment after he claimed he'd found Wong and had seen him getting on a hydrofoil. I passed the information to the Hong Kong Drug Section for their potential follow-up. Gould believed Wong would go to the Philippines, which was the alleged location of his supposed feigned death. For this, Gould was on his own and left to make his own connections, but I requested that he keep me informed.

Another case, dubbed "the Ice Queen," focused on Lee Chau-ping. Staff Sergeants Larry Vander Graaf and Tom Hansen and I worked with the Royal Hong Kong Police to apprehend what turned out to be the largest supplier of methamphetamine ever. I worked closely with Sandy Boucher, a tenacious and professional drug officer capable of overseeing some of the largest trafficking investigations in Asia.

The case all started when I was briefed that Lee and her family were on the run and heading to Canada. Her husband had purchased a restaurant in Saskatchewan and was suspected to already be in Canada. Lee, however, was on a flight due to arrive in Vancouver in ten hours. She was on the run after her methamphetamine factory had been located in China. In an attempt to arrest her upon her arrival, the Vancouver RCMP office and the Canada Border Services Agency were alerted and requested to withhold her landed status. I am really not sure how my very direct message was misinterpreted, but somehow, someone granted her access to Canada. She slipped away.

Due to this oversight, a full investigation was required. Two Vancouver IPOC investigators, Tom Hansen and Larry Vander Graaf, assumed investigative responsibility. Both worked closely with me in Hong Kong, as well as with Sandy Boucher and his team. Despite our in-depth investigation, Lee was not located. It is possible she was hiding out somewhere in Asia.

I also had the occasion to meet with Lam Fuxing, a senior Chinese investigator. We met just inside the Chinese border, and he provided an overview of a factory and the massive potential it had for producing methamphetamine. He also offered me the chance to interview one of the arrestees who he said ran the lab. I declined, knowing that anything that was said would be inadmissible because of the Chinese lack of due process. He informed me that there would not be another opportunity, as all the arrestees would be executed the following day. He added that the cost of the bullet would have to be paid by their families, this without expression or any sense of regard for humanity.

Throughout my three years in Hong Kong, I gained the trust and respect of many of the folks within various units of the RHKP, the Independent Commission Against Corruption, and Her Majesty's Customs and Excise. I learned, in confidence, a profusion of highly sensitive intelligence involving corrupt officials and senior triads, and was provided with a copy of the "triad list" that had been recovered in a police raid. Prior to leaving Hong Kong, I briefed the senior management of the Independent Commission Against Corruption, a briefing that was also shared with the United Kingdom's last governor of Hong Kong, Chris Patten. To have this level of respect bestowed on me was extremely satisfying and made up for the lack of RCMP leadership support.

Chapter Seventeen

SIDEWINDER

In the summer of 1994, having completed my three-year tour, I returned to Canada. It did not initially look like the force was willing to bring me back to Ottawa; a promotion to inspector seemed unlikely. Fortunately, Superintendent Claude Sweeney intervened with Commissioner Joseph Philip Robert Murray and I received the "Commission to Inspector" scroll working under Sweeney's direction. The high commissioner wrote a glowing report to the RCMP commissioner:

> Mr. Clement's success in cultivating his contacts has been dramatically illustrated in his last few weeks here in Hong Kong, where over one hundred senior officers of the Royal Hong Kong Police, the Independent Commission Against Corruption, and the Hong Kong Customs service attended his farewell. He also received specific acknowledgement for his work from the most senior levels of the RHKP, including the commissioner.

I received three letters, which I feel evinced the respect and credibility I had acquired in my three-year tour. Commissioner Donald McFarlane Watson of Customs and Excise wrote:

> I know I speak for my colleagues in Hong Kong Customs and Excise when I say that we will be sorry to see you go. Your tour of duty in Hong Kong has been marked by a very high level of professional cooperation.

Commissioner Li Kwan-ha wrote:

> During the three years that you have served in Hong Kong, you have established a reputation for professionalism and sincerity in your liaison duties. It was indeed a pleasure to have an officer of your calibre available to assist my officers in the many complex matters involving Canada that have arisen during this period.

Finally, Jim Buckle, head of operations for the Independent Commission Against Corruption wrote:

> I should like to take this formal opportunity of thanking you for all you have done for this organization over the past three years or so. I think we have stronger ties with the RCMP today than we have ever had and much of that is due to your endeavours. We are truly grateful.

The only person from the RCMP who acknowledged what I accomplished while in Hong Kong was Deputy Commissioner

Frank Palmer, the same officer who provided background for my rebuttal to Inkster about law school.

Having garnered expertise in Asian-based crime should have been seen as value added within the RCMP; however, rather than capitalize on a three-year "graduate course" through hands-on experience with the RHKP, the force chose to have me transferred to Protective Operations. Although I was extremely grateful for the promotion that was offered thanks to Sweeney and Commissioner Murray, one could argue it was like moving a surgeon to a dental office. This seemed to be the norm in the RCMP and was the eventual reason for its inability to effectively take on major organized financial crime.

The skills acquired by liaison officers stationed overseas need to be capitalized on when these officers return to Canada. And yet, this is seldom the case. What could be construed as a three-to-five-year exchange to augment skills and foster cultural understanding ends up being a wasted opportunity, a solid foundation left to disuse and decay. Not to mention, the expertise of members needs to be respected, as decisions pertaining to areas of concern are best taken when the relevant contextual information provided is based on *actual* experiences and not just intelligence reports. In my case, my transfer once again demonstrated that federal policing was not given the recognition that it demands. Intervention at this stage could have rerouted the influence of China and of Asian-based organized crime. We could have avoided what has since transpired. But whether by design or just pure naïveté, this failure to make good use of human resources has created a huge problem with very little recourse.

The appropriate level of respect was never given to Brian McAdam, who was, in my opinion, the catalyst behind sensitizing Canada to the threat imposed by triads and the inattention of some Canadian officials. The immigration program failed to ensure we kept organized-crime applicants out of Canada, and ignored the warnings and intelligence provided by Brian and me. It was primarily through McAdam's efforts that a project called Sidewinder, involving the RCMP and the Canadian Security Intelligence Service (CSIS), and focusing on the threat of China and the triads, commenced in Canada. It is interesting to note how his report was buried, and how those involved in its creation were chastised. (In Sam Cooper's illuminating book *Wilful Blindness: How a Criminal Network of Narcos, Tycoons, and Chinese Communist Party Agents Infiltrated the West*, Cooper covers this aspect in detail.) The extent of the involvement of triad leaders in Canadian business and in political circles, first revealed in the Sidewinder report, is echoed in Operation Dragon Lord. This sixty-two-page report includes eight pages describing the Canadian situation.[14]

The report cites a troubling example of the close relationship of André Desmarais of Montreal's Power Corporation to the Chinese government through CITIC Pacific (the Hong Kong branch of the company). At this time, Desmarais owned 4 percent of CITIC Pacific's shares. As Michel Juneau-Katsuya, a former CSIS agent, stated:

> Our government, like so many governments around the world, have begun to think like large corporations, to see that its ultimate responsibility is to the bottom line. It is because of this . . . that the Canadian government blindly, despite all the warning signs, continues to foster ever-increasing ties to the Chinese government.

We have seen this repeatedly with former prime ministers. Peter Harder (now Senator Harder) was the impetus behind sidelining Brian McAdam, which also resulted in CSIS and the RCMP dropping the investigation. The report was buried. No potential investigations were commenced to halt Chinese espionage and corruption of officials—and the responsibility for that inaction rests at the feet of the government in power at the time, commencing with Pierre Elliott Trudeau's administration, up to and inclusive of Chrétien's. By keeping their heads in the sand, they are responsible for what has transpired involving China. China has taken advantage of Canada, which not only damages our country but also negatively impacts the Chinese diaspora in Canada. Events like the bankruptcy of Nortel, clearly contrived by Chinese espionage activities, should have alerted our political masters to the repercussions of overlooking what the Sidewinder report had made obvious.

The Sidewinder report highlighted how the Chinese Communist Party has infiltrated many aspects of Canadian society. Nortel is a perfect example of this. It has been well established that intellectual property was stolen and duplicated in China, which eventually resulted in the company's demise. Canadian leaders, elite Canadians, and some of our most powerful corporations have pushed for closer ties with China. Canada's elite relationship with China goes back to the tenure of Prime Minister Pierre Elliott Trudeau. One of Trudeau's main foreign policies was to strengthen ties with China and help bring them into the United Nations. In his early days, he was an activist from Quebec who had visited China in 1949, and again in 1960 prior to becoming prime minister. In 1973, when he visited China as prime minister, he praised China for its governance. In my view, this was the beginning of the "open arms" relationship Canadian leaders have cultivated with China.

The Canada China Business Council (CCBC), founded by Paul Desmarais (André's father) of Power Corp., paved the way for many of the relationships that were fostered with China. Of interest, and possibly disconcerting, is the fact that former prime ministers Paul Martin, Jean Chrétien, and Brian Mulroney all had a tight relationship with the CCBC and Power Corp.[15] One could draw an analogy that working either directly or indirectly with the CCBC was a retirement career choice for our prime ministers. According to a statement in Jonathan Manthorpe's *Claws of the Panda: Beijing's Campaign of Influence and Intimidation in Canada*, the CCBC "became a persuasive lobby for enhanced relations with China, where the benefits of trade were held to be of paramount concern."

One of the powerful Chinese leaders who supported the CCBC was Bo Xilai. During my tenure at Pace Global Advantage, a trip was organized to China wherein Bo Xilai was the main host. Former immigration minister Sergio Marchi was also on contract with PGA helped arrange meetings. A short while after the visit, Bo's wife, Gu Kailai, was arrested for the murder of a British businessman, and Bo was linked to the harvesting of organs from Falun Dafa prisoners of conscience. Reflecting on Lam Fuxing's statement when he explained that prisoners would be shot with bullets bought by their family members, this supports what has been rumoured for years: that China does not value the lives of its citizens.

Prior to the conclusion of the Sidewinder review, senior management in the force asked me to share my views. I expressed that the investigation was warranted and that our having assigned a corporal with little to no experience to delve into the allegations was, in and of itself, criminal. This was not received in a positive light.

If we were to ask ourselves why Sidewinder was axed, it could be argued that trade and the political belief that we should extend open arms to China were more important than the negative consequences being experienced today, e.g., the fentanyl crisis. But neither the RCMP's senior management nor CSIS's senior management were willing to take a stand and speak for what was right; rather than take action to ensure Sidewinder was fully explored and that, where necessary, investigations followed, they allowed Chinese influence to rule the day.

Over the years and to this day, we have seen extensive money laundering from China into Canada. In 2020, the Province of British Columbia established the Cullen Commission, which has a mandate to investigate the money-laundering problem in British Columbia—a problem that, thanks to investigative reporters, was making the news almost daily.[16] The commission's conclusion explains the genesis of many of the money-laundering issues, and has enabled Canada to become somewhat aware of the effects of our inattention toward China. Most recently we have seen news reports about illegal Chinese police stations being set up within Chinese Canadian communities with the goal of keeping emigrated Chinese people loyal to China.[17] Additionally, we have witnessed China achieve its goal, first proposed in 2013, of establishing its Belt and Road Initiative, a global infrastructure development strategy with connections and influence around the world.[18] The current opioid overdose epidemic directly relates to precursor chemicals flowing out of China. Vancouver has become a transshipment point for many drugs entering North America. Much like the UK's open-door philosophy to Russian oligarchs, Canada has failed to heed the predicted impact of an open relationship with China.

There is ample evidence to show that the opioid overdose epidemic has a direct correlation to China and the triads. My argument in the nineties that Vancouver would become a transshipment point for drugs coming out of Asia has played out as I forecasted. North American's federal law-enforcement inaction in the nineties has created the reality we are witnessing today. But governments argued that trade with China was paramount. Greed trumped ethics.

I have recently given interviews with the Australian Broadcasting Corporation focusing on casinos in Australia and their infiltration and ownership by known triad figures. Following the growing media attention, the Australian government ordered an inquiry that mirrors what we witnessed in the Cullen Commission. Recently, the *Financial Times*, in conjunction with the Royal United Services Institute (a UK-based think tank), revealed that well-known business figures in East Asia linked to organized crime have helped facilitate illicit deliveries of hundreds of thousands of barrels of oil to North Korea. The deliveries to North Korea were connected to a Hong Kong trader linked both to the triads and to a former gambling tycoon currently serving time for his triad activities. China's sanctioning of this activity is strongly suspected, which should serve as an indicator of how far China is prepared to go in their quest around the world.

China, under the Chinese Communist Party, is essentially a criminal organization that represents a fundamental challenge to lawful societies around the world. I firmly believe that any dealings with China must be measured in the context of that country's real agenda. We have known for years that Chinese students submit intelligence briefs back to China. We know that there are a number of Chinese landed immigrants who help the Chinese government maintain some control on the Chinese diaspora. I have recently heard statements by acquaintances I have spoken with on panels that if we were to have a conflict with China, we could find ourselves with a large percentage of some Chinese immigrants siding with China.

At the time of completing my writing of this book, my RCMP team were exposed to a report that former inspector Bill Majcher was allegedly co-opted to assist China in tracking people thought to be Chinese fraudsters. It needs to be understood is that there is no rule of law there, so whether there was actually fraud or whether evidence of such was fabricated for the benefit of the China's leadership is debatable.[19]

One interesting investigation involving Bill Majcher when he was still an undercover operator for the RCMP was a case dubbed "the Bermuda Short." I had known Bill several years prior to this case and felt he was extremely bright, with impressive knowledge of the stock market, but needed to be strongly controlled to ensure that investigations he participated in could meet any legal challenges.

The Bermuda Short involved working with the FBI in Florida. Twenty Canadians were caught in the undercover sting. Several of the Canadians had regulatory convictions. Some had criminal convictions ranging from charges for trafficking in cocaine to expulsion from the Institute of Chartered Accountants of British Columbia for defrauding clients.

I was in Florida at the time of the arrests and represented the RCMP at a joint FBI-RCMP press conference. The FBI agent, Ross Gaffney, managed all the indictments in Florida. I got to know Ross well in later years when I ran my investigative practice. The investigation was solid, but Majcher was not—it was found he'd been sleeping with the judge who was handling the trial.

Majcher approached me prior to my retirement to support him for a "commission rank," that of inspector. I told him I could not in good faith support him as I didn't feel he was objective enough to lead investigators. My superior apparently felt otherwise and promoted Majcher to inspector (I'd already left the RCMP by that point). Majcher lasted only a short time in that role.

He moved to Hong Kong, where he operated an investigative and consulting business. I met him once in Hong Kong in 2013; I was working with HSBC in a training capacity. Majcher boasted that he was doing extremely well and had many prominent clients.

Most recently, Majcher was charged for allegedly helping Communist China with files involving Chinese Canadians. Unfortunately, it appears he roped in my very good friends Kim Marsh and Ross Gaffney. The outcome has yet to be written, but I am a firm believer that the truth will absolve Kim and Ross.

Chapter Eighteen

INTEGRATED PROCEEDS OF
CRIME (IPOC)

Upon my return to Canada, I was transferred to Protective Operations. This role was at the furthest point from my expertise, but it provided the RCMP and the Canadian government an opportunity to help prepare cost-saving measures for a study being undertaken by the commissioner. As a result, I wrote myself out of a position and needed to find another home. Not being someone to rely on the organization to manage my career, I quickly realized that the Proceeds of Crime unit in the National Capital Region would be elevated to an Integrated Proceeds of Crime unit and therefore I could become an inspector. After lobbying with the national officer in charge of Proceeds of Crime as well as with Division management, I assumed the role. I held this role for eight years, working with many committed and dedicated police personnel from various police services: Ottawa Police, Sûreté du Québec, Ontario Provincial Police, and other federal government departments including the Department of Justice, the Canada Revenue Agency, and the Canada Border Services Agency.

Shortly after my arrival, I was pulled away from the unit to assist in the internal review of the 24 Sussex incident involving Prime Minister Chrétien and his wife, Aline. The commanding officer directed me to undertake an independent investigation. My immediate goal was to secure the security videotapes, which would be housed in the security huts. The video clearly showed an intruder, but dishearteningly, the member on duty had reset the video without investigating. In fact, one of the members, while speaking to a colleague in the security hut at the governor general's residence, heard glass break but took no action. The intruder was on the grounds for a minimum of forty-five minutes. With tapes in hand, I returned and briefed senior command, resulting in my being temporarily assigned to work with Chief Superintendent Wayne Martell to provide a report for presentation to the commissioner and solicitor general.

The event reminds me of when I did my short stint as a sergeant with Protective Ops and commented about the level of protection we offered our prime minister. The members were special constables who received only a fraction of the training of a regular member. At the time, special constables did not receive the full Regina training at the Depot detachment, but instead completed a course designed to train them to be protective officers. Well, for this 24 Sussex incident, the low standards I'd witnessed with Protective Ops were belly to the ground—when the alarm was tripped, the special constables took not one prudent action. I told Martell that I felt my young daughters would have been more responsive. And while the corporal who was on duty overseeing the special constables reacted appropriately, time was allowed for the perpetrator to get into the residence. When Mrs. Chrétien called the guardhouse, the on-premises members surrounded the house but did nothing until the corporal arrived. Lack of judgment, of initiative—in short, the group was weak.

During the review I found that the procedure only required the members to alert the regular members who were patrolling all VIP locations. This was an oversight on the part of leadership.

The first action was to bring members to Ottawa from across the country to replace the special constables who were presently occupying positions. The next action was to appoint an inspector—my recommendation won the day. While at 24 Sussex two days later, Prime Minister Chrétien approached me and asked if the new bodies were real police officers. In light of what had occurred, it was a fair question.

As occurs in any major event when the force fails to act appropriately, heads must roll. This case was no different. A few members were transferred into to non-operational roles, but senior leadership was spared.

Over my eight years in the IPOC unit, we investigated and prosecuted multiple proceeds-of-crime-and-money-laundering cases, most of which resulted in guilty pleas due to the professional documentation. A few cases stood out and, dare I say, caused a lot of angst and a few scars.

As a result of the severity of the damage of the ice storm in 1998, I was able to get support to assist citizens in the outlying areas after some impassioned discussions with the commanding officer. The farming community in and around Metcalfe, Ontario, were desperate, so, through my brother Bob, we got a tractor-trailer load of generators. My brother arrived at Donevelyn Farms with a military escort, and the generators were managed for distribution by the farm. We worked late into the night and most of those present were aware of what I did, so they started speaking to me about the local community. Some asked why we'd never investigated Sandy Wammes, who was known to them as a large-scale cocaine trafficker.

Once back in the office, I assigned John Sullivan and Jacques Beaulieu to conduct a background on Wammes with the intent of making this a project. Within a year we made a number of arrests and seized property. Then, in late 2014, Wammes was arrested *again* by the OPP in a large-scale drug investigation. Some people never learn.

In January 1996 a decision was taken to target Flint Kaya, a bar owner in Hull, Quebec, notorious for drug trafficking and, according to several sources, sexually assaulting his waitresses. There were also disconcerting allegations of a senior Ottawa Police officer associating with Kaya.

When I received the allegations in writing from one of my Ottawa Police Service members attached to the unit, I raised my concerns with the criminal operations officer and the commanding officer. Although they were not initially forthcoming, I explained that we held an intelligence file on this matter and had become aware of these allegations several months before. After some pressure from me, they provided me with the file. The commanding officer told me that if I took this on, it would be at my peril.

This episode again made evident the need for an independent body to undertake corruption investigations involving public officials. The fact that a file existed and yet no action had been taken serves to demonstrate that many police leaders remain heedless of what is in front of them. Rather than act, they remain silent until it blows up. As many police leaders used to say: Avoid operations until unavoidable, and then don't take on anything controversial. Just stay out of trouble and remain promotable.

As the jurisdiction for corruption in Ontario rested with the Ontario Provincial Police, I contacted Chief Superintendent Wayne Frechette, whom I knew well, and after I was briefed, we reached an agreement to undertake a joint investigation, with the OPP responsible for the corruption allegation, and our unit responsible for Flint Kaya.

We gathered evidence using a series of agents, having one of them travel with Kaya to Montreal. That agent obtained two ounces of cocaine from an alleged twelve-kilo supply. To provide the agent with the credibility to be able to purchase large quantities, the decision was made to allow the agent to introduce the U/C persona I was using in the Larry Miller investigation (which I will describe in detail in the next chapter).

The investigation resulted in the arranged purchase of a kilo of cocaine for $36,000, which was to be handled by the agent, and a second undercover operator introduced as my runner. At this time, we also learned that Kaya's brother was running drugs for Andrew Scoppa, a confidante of Vito Rizzuto (the alleged leader of the Sicilian organized-crime group in Canada, who'd broken his oath of secrecy to speak to journalists).

This investigation had more twists and turns than any I had ever been involved with. We ended up signing several agents, all of whom provided evidence of Kaya's past and present criminal activities. The main agent was going to purchase drugs directly from Kaya and one of his waitresses was going to testify in the sexual-assault case. In 1996, Kaya was arrested for sexual assault and was subsequently released on bail.

At this time, I was also engaged, again, in a high-level organized-crime undercover operation involving the US and Canada but was mandated to manage my unit and the Kaya investigation at the same time. The U/C I was involved in played a significant role in bringing the Kaya matter to a close. I was able to use my persona to contact Kaya through the agent to place a multi-kilo cocaine order, which ultimately led to Andrew Scoppa.

This investigation culminated with both Kaya and Scoppa being charged with conspiracy to traffic. An Ottawa Police inspector was also charged, but the charge was later dismissed in court following the retraction of an agent's testimony. This retraction only occurred after the officer's lawyer had been permitted by the Crown to meet with him alone.

Kaya dragged the preliminary hearing out for three years and threatened several members, including myself, during this process. His delays resulted in a change of venue to Montreal, and the trial judge blamed the Crown for the lack of expediency in the trial. As a result, Scoppa cut a deal to have Kaya plead to two years' penitentiary time; Scoppa would pay a heavy fine and stay out of jail. It was rationalized that the evidence against Scoppa was circumstantial, and the agents, weak, one of whom was determined to be unreliable. Given that the trial judge was predisposed against giving Kaya additional jail time, this was the best possible all-around outcome.

Decades later, in February 2022, Scoppa was murdered at the Sheraton in Montreal.

This case demonstrates how a major criminal can use stall tactics, such as firing his counsel over and over, that result in a delayed process, with the Crown bearing the wrath of the court. In my view, the judges need to take control of these trials to ensure they move forward whether or not the accused is attempting to thwart the process. I was interviewed at the end of the trial, and I remarked that it was time judges took control of their courtrooms. As you can appreciate, all hell broke loose. The commissioner received a call from the minister of justice, which made its way down to me. I simply repeated to my senior command that this multimillion-dollar investigation had been foiled by the accused, while the court neglected to use strong direction to maintain the expediency and integrity of the process. Our dissatisfaction should have been expressed publicly, not by me, but by senior command.

Chapter Nineteen

THE LARRY MILLER OPERATION

As I mentioned in the previous chapter, during the Kaya investigation I was also involved in a high-level undercover smuggling operation. Prior to this, our unit had looked into the ongoing transfer of money via Brink's truck from Jefferson National Bank in Massena, New York, to Royal Bank (RBC) on Sparks Street in Ottawa. At this time, smuggling had not been brought into the proceeds-of-crime regime, so RBC willingly accepted the transfer of millions of dollars in Canadian currency that came through smuggling. We were confidentially provided correspondence that showed the bank's senior managers were well aware of the money's origins, so I delved into all the possibilities through which we might hold RBC to account. Unfortunately, when smuggling was brought in as a predicate offence it was not retroactive, thus we could not bring charges to RBC.

What we were able to do, however, was to delve further into investigating the organizations who were using Jefferson National Bank. One name kept surfacing: Larry Miller. We had an individual who was willing to become an agent and introduce an RCMP member into the Miller organization, and the profile for this operation fit my background well: older and with international experience in organized crime and money laundering. With what I believed was the blessing of the commanding officers of both Ontario and the National Capital Region, I agreed to undertake the operation and provide salient advice on how to move forward with the investigation.

The agent was Cal Broeker, subject of the true-crime book *Smokescreen: One Man Against the Underworld* by Paul William Roberts and Norman Snider, an account of Cal's undercover work for the RCMP. Cal's credentials as a businessman operating as a shipping broker were well established, so his ability to introduce an operator was straightforward. In *Smokescreen*, I am described as follows:

> The cop looked a great deal younger than his forty-eight years. Darkly handsome, he'd grown a goatee, and had his hair layered short and spiky. The clothes were right too: flashy but expensive. It all said taste and money, and a taste for money is what criminals have in common.

To strengthen my story, we established RGW Trucking, the initials of my undercover name: Robert "Bob" Gordon Williams. I relied heavily on my youngest brother, who had run a trucking company for years, to help me to appear to be in the truck business. His expertise was invaluable. Thanks to his ongoing crucial advice I was able to ensure that our shipments went across the border relatively unimpeded. Although the most senior levels of Canada Border Services had been briefed, it was not possible to brief anyone on the front lines since we knew that Miller had co-opted agents on the American side. The team did an impeccable job of setting up an office with all the trappings of a legitimate business. The driver for the transport was a trained, qualified U/C operator who fit the profile.

Larry Miller had been convicted of armed robbery in 1967, and there are allegations he had some limited ties to the Genovese crime family. At the time of our investigation, he was a notable high roller in Las Vegas. He had access to a Learjet, which he used to fly from Vegas to Massena, where he owned Club 37 and a fully paid $200,000 home. He also owned a home in Vegas. The Miller organization allegedly made six to eight hundred million dollars between 1992 and 1996.

The organization included the following people. In Massena, New York:

- Nick Miller, Larry's son.
- Victoria Miller Glines, Larry's daughter.
- Timothy Glines, Victoria's husband.
- Shawn Burke, the alleged front man, and Nick Miller's best friend.

In Las Vegas, Nevada:

- Richard "Dick" Rancati, Larry's right-hand man with a mafia connection to the Genovese crime family in New Jersey.
- In Cornwall, Ontario:
- Rick Kalil and John Ciarlo, both believed to be associated to the Zappia crime family in Ottawa.

The Zappia family was part of the Sicilian organized-crime group that had emigrated to Canada and had associations with Frank Cotroni, who was involved in a massive fraud during the 1976 building of the Olympic Village in Montreal. He along with many other notable crime figures had influence over many of the construction unions in Ontario and Quebec. Neither Kalil nor Ciarlo were in his league; rather, they came across as being nothing more than introducers and hangers-on who'd reap whatever funds got thrown their way. Ciarlo could've been an extra in *The Sopranos*. He got angry at me once when I commented that his toupée looked like roadkill. Larry laughed extensively.

Frank Miller's assets included:

- a house in Massena valued at $240,000;
- a residence in Las Vegas valued at $470,000;
- Club 37 in Massena, valued at $280,000;
- two lots on the St. Lawrence River valued $50,000 each;
- another lot next to the residence of Shawn Burke valued at $50,000;
- a second property in Las Vegas;
- a third Vegas property valued at $500,000;
- at the beginning of the project, a Learjet valued at $2,000,000;
- several companies, including LBL Imports/Exports, VTN in the US, and Advanced Construction Technologies in Russia;
- investments in Arizona Charlie's in Las Vegas;
- a plethora of bank accounts in various institutions;
- an alleged investment of $20,000,000 in a Russian casino project.

He was also suspected to have had bank accounts in Antigua, Bermuda, Grand Cayman, England, and Switzerland, and we believed that he used many of his associates to conceal other assets. He definitely used nominees for registering his vehicles, such as his girlfriend, Tony Chase, and his son-in-law, Tim Glines.

One of our agents secured the operation's success when they were contacted in 1995 by Rick Kalil. Kalil inquired if the agent could assist the Miller group in diverting product from the US into Canada. The agent had previously spent time in Bulgaria and was familiar with international trade and banking. The agent was introduced to the Miller group via Shawn Burke.

Organized-crime groups always have an Achilles' heel. In Frank Miller's case, it was the need to get alcohol and cigarettes out of the US and into Canada. This was done under the guise of moving the shipments offshore to divert shipments to clients in Ontario and BC. That is where we came in. We had a trucking company, so relying on Cal Broeker's international experience and on his verifiable guise of an offshore outlet made us a prime resource for Miller.

From December 1995 to February 1996, Broeker met with members of the Miller organization four times. Larry told him that his organization could supply five hundred thousand dollars of contraband (alcohol and tobacco) per week. In March 1996, Dick Rancati suggested to Broeker that he establish a trucking company that would be bonded, and that he place a pro forma order to VTN Inc., which stood for Vicki, Tim, and Nick (Larry's daughter, son-in-law, and son), requesting prepayment. Rancati further directed Broeker to order 1600 cases of liquor at $32,780 USD.

Later in March, there was a meeting with the agent where Shawn Burke, Rick Kalil, John Ciarlo, and Larry Miller were present. Miller provided funds for the order as directed above. As a result of this meeting, Kalil, Ciarlo, and Burke met the agent, and a call was placed between Kalil and me. I was polite during the call but explained that I did not know Kalil and would be more comfortable if I met directly with Larry.

In April, Rancati and Burke met with the agent again, pressuring him to get moving on the loads. Rancati emphasized his mob connections and that he could get other deals if the agent was interested.

On April 25, I met with Burke, Rancati, and the agent in Montreal. After a lengthy discussion, in which Rancati warned that if anything were to happen to Larry, I would pay for it, we reached an agreement to move the first load and that Burke would meet me in Cornwall to make payment. Rancati confirmed he would move the liquor from the US warehouse to Detroit, where we could pick up the load.

On May 15, the first load of alcohol was obtained in the US. When the U/C operator was stopped at the border, he called me and said that there was a problem. I was near the border, so I met with the Canada Border Services officer, who asked about certain mandatory forms. I pretended that I had to make a call and contacted my brother Bob. Within fifteen minutes Bob sufficiently briefed me on the requirements such that I was able to speak with some authority to the officer. My answers must have satisfied her, as she enabled the load to move forward.

We drove the load, per Miller's instructions, to a predetermined warehouse in Hamilton, Ontario. We met with Burke, Kalil, Scott Kimble, and Brent Maxwell. Inside the warehouse were a number of rental trucks. I took detailed notes on my laptop as I sat in my vehicle, noting all the licence numbers, which I then passed to the cover team located in the area. Brent Maxwell provided Burke with a bag of money and then I was paid a total of $54,500. The payment consisted of $27,500 in cash for delivering and $27,000 to be wired to VTN's US account.

On May 17, Burke and Rancati met with me at the bogus trucking-company office. We confirmed a second order. Throughout the meeting, I made it appear as though I was answering calls from truckers working for "my company," and in a loud enough voice for my guests to hear, I expressed displeasure that "the monies" had not been picked up—all to open the conversation about my ability to launder money.

On May 21, Rancati and Burke came to the office again to meet with me. They informed me that the bank accounts had been switched from LBL to VTN. Rancati called Vicky and had her generate paperwork to justify the shipment.

On May 23, there was a second shipment. Again, the delivery was made to a warehouse in Hamilton where Burke and Leslie "Les" Maxwell, Brent's father, were present. Interestingly, when I told them I was shortchanged on the amount they paid me for the previous trip, they made it up and provided $64,500 this time around.

On May 25 in Massena at Larry Miller's Club 37, I was introduced to Larry. Nick Miller inquired whether I would transport cigarettes from Florida to New Jersey and then Larry added that he also needed someone to smuggle items into Russia. He asked, too, about getting a tobacco shipment into Vancouver.

From May 25 to 29, there were a number of phone meetings focusing on delays in documents and fleshing out Larry's requested items. I received a call from a customs broker, Joe Lutheran, that the next shipment would be delayed until May 31. When that day came, a third shipment was picked up and delivered to Neo Industries Limited in Hamilton, a warehouse whose location made it possible for the alcohol to be unloaded out of sight. Again, I recorded the rental trucks' licence numbers as, at this point, the project team was arranging for some of the smaller shipments to be intercepted by officers once they were away from the warehouse. Three people were arrested.

On June 3, there was a meeting in Ottawa with Kalil and Ciarlo, who inquired about getting some loads delivered there. The agent had a call with Larry, who was pushing to have vodka delivered to Russia.

On June 4, another meeting in Ottawa, this time with Burke, Ciarlo, and Kalil. There was concern about the arrests in Hamilton. Larry had allegedly contacted USDP to confirm that the load could not be traced back to him. In order to minimize potential blowback, I told him I had a source in the Hamilton Police Service and would make some inquiries.

On June 7, I met Burke and Nick Miller at Club 37. We discussed the shipment of cigarettes from Florida to New Jersey with a final destination being the Akwesasne Reserve. Miller explained we would need to do it in six shipments.

On June 18, a fourth load of alcohol was picked up in Detroit, driven to Hamilton, and unloaded at Douglas Samson's farm. The cover team's cars were spotted, so I told everyone I had some of my people "on the inside" doing counter-surveillance; this went over very well and was judged to be a wise move. I also insinuated that my police source had told me there was a leak in Hamilton and that is what caused the previous seizure. Burke turned over $64,500 in cash.

By this point in the operation, senior managers in London were becoming concerned with the amount of product being permitted to make it to the street. This concern resulted in delays in receiving authority sanction to move forward, an uncomfortable position to be in when you as the operator are the one having to continually make excuses for those delays. On June 20, there was supposed to be another meeting in Ottawa; Burke, Kalil, and Ciarlo had gone to the office. As there was nothing but procrastination coming from senior management in regard to what to agree to for future loads, my frustration set in, and I called the commanding officer of the time, Giuliano "Zack" Zaccardelli, directly. He was clearly not happy with that, but thankfully, we were given instruction to proceed.

What has never ceased to amaze me is that senior leaders apparently fail to realize that they expose undercover operators to potential risk when they play armchair quarterback and become risk averse. Dealing with organized crime–affiliated individuals is not something to be taken lightly, and yet senior managers who have never been in an undercover role fail to grasp the dangers associated with their inaction.

Undercover operators constantly have to negotiate and arrange meetings with individuals who are capable of murder. It is essential that we maintain credibility and avoid continually stalling on agreed-to meetings and transactions. You can only make so many excuses before raising alarm bells with the criminal organization.

I told Zack that if they did not want to move forward, I would return to my unit, which I also had to manage. I knew that it would come back to bite me (and it did, later on, when I was being considered for promotion), but his failure to support our efforts in tackling the Miller case still surprised me somewhat, seeing as Zack had spoken of his desire to focus on organized crime.

So, the meeting went ahead. We discussed the Vancouver shipment of cigarettes and finalized the next load of alcohol. Kalil also wanted three loads of cigarettes, which would need to be delivered in three different Canadian cities to Asian players. Another meeting was held at Club 37 on June 25 with Larry Miller, Burke, and the agent. The logistics of the Vancouver shipment were fleshed out and the next alcohol deliveries were confirmed for June 27 and September 9.

The fifth load was picked up and delivered to a chicken farm owned by Tommy Jacobs. Leslie Maxwell gave Burke $61,100, which in turn was passed to me. I documented the trucks' licence numbers, and as I had done previously, complained about a miscount. In reply, Burke confirmed he would make up the difference on the next payment. The count had, in fact, always been correct, but they did not have a good grasp on their finances.

On July 3, I wired $25,774 to Northwest Bank in Minnesota to pay for the load scheduled for July 9, which was picked up and taken to Tommy's farm. Les Maxwell gave Burke $62,400, and this was passed to me. When the shipment left in smaller loads using the rental vehicles, two people were arrested.

On July 11, another $25,774 was wired to a bank in Minnesota as payment for a load July 16. The seventh load was picked up and delivered to the residence of C. Kaarsemaker. Brent Maxwell gave Burke four hundred dollars to give to me to make up for short-changing me on the last shipment, and then Les Maxwell give Burke $62,000.

On July 18, there was a meeting in Ottawa with Rancati, Nick Miller, and Burke. Rancati spoke about having access to German war bonds that had been held by his organized-crime contacts; he wanted to move them for a fraction of their value. I agreed to look into it. Nick asked about getting liquor delivered to Hogansburg, New York, for the Reserve. I also had a long discussion with Burke about his need to do a better job concealing his wealth, and that I could help conceal his assets and provide offshore money-laundering facilities.

On July 22, Rancati called and arranged for a meeting with Larry to discuss the Vancouver cigarette shipment. Burke also called me to discuss me laundering $350,000 to start. Then another call from Rancati, inquiring about my cost to convert $1,250,000 into US dollars. We met at Club 37. Larry, Nick, Burke, and Rancati were present. We ironed out more details on the cigarette shipment, learning that Nick and Shawn would be in Vancouver. Nick brought up the conversion of the $1,250,000, and confirmed it was his money. We discussed the German war bonds, but by this time it was confirmed that they were worthless.

On August 1, Burke called about laundering his $350,000 but explained that the money was not available just yet. He said Larry wanted to split the cigarette load to reduce the financial risk, to which I responded that splitting actually created more risk.

On August 21, we met once again at Club 37. Due to the arrests stemming from the Hamilton loads and my feigning that I had knowledge of a leak on the Maxwells' end, we decided to postpone any further Hamilton loads. Burke indicated the next load would need to be delivered to Picton, Ontario.

On August 28, Larry, Burke, Rancati, and I met at Club 37. Much of our discussion focused on "the Hamilton situation." I told Larry that I had a contact at the IRS and could, for a fee, check out whether there was any "heat" on him. Larry also spoke about his direct connections with Philip Morris and how they often frequented Sonora Resort in BC for meetings. He insinuated an invite might be coming my way.

During this same trip to Massena, Burke took me around to show me his assets: a small hobby farm, a cigar boat, a '57 Thunderbird, and a "Fatboy" Harley. I suggested we needed to get these out of his name to protect them in the event of arrests, also that he draw up a will and that I would do him the favour of arranging it when I started laundering his money.

On September 7, I attended Burke's birthday party. His wife and his wife's parents were present. Burke stressed that I not mention anything about our business during the party. When he introduced me to his wife, I said that if anything were to ever happen to him, I would look after his wife, and he laughed.

On September 10, Burke and Nick Miller met at my office in Nepean, at which time Burke warned me that during his birthday party, his First Nations contacts had intercepted certain conversations. I had been wearing a transmitting device at the party, and so naturally found this info very disconcerting. In the United States, law enforcement undercover agents must have their conversations with criminal organizations recorded; concealed transmitting devices are therefore the rule of the day. I was surprised that the device the US authorities had provided was so poor that its signals could be picked up so easily by outside individuals. I joked that it was likely just some calls picked up and nothing to be worried about, and this seemed to satisfy them. But the only reason they didn't reject that flimsy answer was the depth of the relationship that had been forged by this point in the operation. I will admit, my heart did skip a few beats. We then finalized arrangements for the cigarette delivery in BC.

The Attorney General of the day in BC refused to authorize any of the cigarettes for distribution, so the shipment had to be seized once delivered. On September 18, the cover team and I arrived in BC and briefed our BC counterparts. September 19, I met with Nick and Burke and was introduced to someone at a warehouse. I told them I didn't like the location, so a second location was identified.

On September 20 I inspected a second warehouse in Richmond. Although the warehouse was far too open and visible to other businesses, which I complained about to Nick and Burke, they opted to proceed. The cigarettes were delivered and I had the operator/driver keep the trailer tight to the warehouse door until the money arrived. Miller gave me $44,980. Immediately following payment, the arrest teams arrived.

I took off in my vehicle and called Larry right away, saying it was bad and that his kids would not listen to me when I said it was too risky of a location. We made it look like I helped get Nick and Burke released, which provided tremendous credibility to my position. (We'd made arrangements to have an RCMP member act as a lawyer and make it appear that they were released because of my support.)

I let on that I drove back to Ontario to avoid any potential arrest, so Larry and I were not in contact again until September 22. It was then that I learned that Larry wanted to get another two loads of alcohol delivered to offset the cigarette loss.

We held a meeting in October at the Ottawa office with Burke and Nick Miller. Miller wanted two loads of liquor delivered to Toronto and another load of cigarettes to BC. On October 17, the agent and Nick met in Cornwall and the agent received $27,000 for the next load. This was followed by another meeting with Nick and Burke, in which details were finalized for a liquor delivery to the Maxwells in Hamilton.

On October 23, 1996, "D-Day," the alcohol was picked up. Burke, Nick Miller, and Scott Kimble were arrested along with Brent and Bob Maxwell. At this time my true identity was revealed.

Arrest warrants were issued for Larry Miller and the other co-conspirators, with their arrests to follow in the coming days.

Larry Miller passed away on July 6, 2012. He had been fighting cancer at the time of the operation.

The success of this operation resulted in the civil actions taken by the Government of Canada against Philip Morris. The case was handled by Greg West in Syracuse, New York. Prior to the arrests, we had discussed the potential sharing of future asset seizures. Up to this point, we had shared all of our evidence, since we were working hand in hand with our American law-enforcement colleagues. But despite the great expense associated with our side of the operation and the risk taken by Canadians to infiltrate the organization, a decision was made that our evidence was not required and therefore only minimal assets would be provided to Canada.

Cigarette and alcohol smuggling continue to occur; they are the direct result of high government taxes. When marijuana was legalized, one of the statements Minister Bill Blair made was that this would reduce organized crime's involvement. But our history with alcohol and tobacco smuggling should have shown that heavy taxes on marijuana would sustain an ongoing criminal market. Legalization was not necessarily the wrong approach, but adding heavy taxes does nothing to thwart organized crime.

On November 11, 1999, at the conclusion of the Flint Kaya and Larry Miller investigations, an informant shared that there was a possible threat against me, allegedly taken out by Kaya and some Russians. This was corroborated by Andrew Scoppa.

At one point, my daughters were being escorted to school, while I was permitted to carry my firearm at all times. Although no definitive information disproved the threat, eventually, it was for all intents and purposes forgotten about. I would like to be able to say that this had no lasting repercussions for my daughters, but any psychologist worth their salt would refute such a claim. For several weeks after the investigations ended, both of my girls looked over their shoulders and carefully regarded any vehicle that slowed down near our home—and we lived on a corner with a stop sign. It's possible this was far harder on me than it was on them, as I blamed myself for bringing this home. I felt a tremendous guilt for a very long time. At no time did anyone from the RCMP ask how I or my family was doing.

Part Six

ON MY WAY OUT

Chapter Twenty

ABC—"ANYONE BUT CLEMENT"

Following the end of the Larry Miller operation, the national director position for Proceeds of Crime opened up. I was one of the most qualified in Canada for that job. And yet, I was passed over. I appealed, and as a result, there was a meeting between Deputy Commissioner René Charbonneau, Officer in Staffing Cal Corley, a lawyer named John Dickson (my representative), and myself. I was shocked by Charbonneau's statement that my having done the undercover operation did not reflect leadership. The operation had resulted in another threat negatively impacting my family, so I was stunned by his position, to say the least. After a lengthy discussion, John observed to the group that it was clearly "ABC"—Anyone but Clement.

This was a hard pill to swallow. It showed me how little respected members who stayed in operations, working hand in hand with investigators, truly were. Yet, my operations team saw my actions as demonstrating the highest standards of leadership: not only did I undertake the Miller operation, but I also simultaneously oversaw the Kaya investigation and other active files within my unit.

During Commissioner Murray's tenure, considerable efforts were made to create focus groups engaging constables and non-commissioned officers, but no thought was given to meeting with the inspector/superintendent cadre, the group that predominantly oversaw the force's operations. So, a group of us spoke out, resulting in the creation of the inspector/superintendent focus group. Commissioner Murray saw this as a positive step and invited a representative to sit in on the senior executive meetings. I was elected by the group to take on this responsibility.

I performed this role for over six years. Sadly, from the time I took on the role, my performance appraisals took a dive. Many senior officers resented the fact that our group existed. At the senior executive committee (SEC) meetings, I witnessed Commissioner Murray being extremely proactive and open-minded. But beyond those meetings, he relied on his senior team, many of whom were unfortunately stuck in the past. When Commissioner Zaccardelli replaced Murray, the first message I received from his office was that he would no longer entertain our inspector/superintendent group—we were no longer invited to SEC meetings. Stubborn me, I refused to step down, and continued to support my colleagues in as many ways as I could.

During this period, I also went through the process to become chief superintendent, which involved appearing before a panel of senior officers and undergoing an intensive interview to test that I was ready for a senior-management role. The commanding officer of the day was unsupportive. It shocked him that I passed with flying colours. I had put in the effort knowing it was only to satisfy myself, since "ABC" was, to my detriment, alive and well.

Following Dawson Hovey's transfer into the commanding officer position, he suggested I needed to resign as the officer representative, since I would never be promoted as long as I remained in that position. He felt that "the force was not mature enough to deal with such a program." I had a great deal of respect for Hovey and realized he was unfortunately right. The force still expected military-style obedience and cultish loyalty. Speaking out was frowned upon—it was practically a punishable offence to speak truth to power. This has been a problem in the RCMP.

Being as close to HQ as I was, I witnessed officers who had not been in an operational role for years receiving promotions over and over again, and as such, their total operational experience was sadly lacking. What was the obvious route to professional gain? Playing politics, staying out of operations, and lauding your boss. But one thing I've always said: you should be able to look in the mirror and be happy with what you see.

Experienced officers were needed to provide training in financial crime to various countries. As the RCMP's IPOC model was being held out as a best practice, there was no shortage of international requests. Since I had remained in the Proceeds of Crime investigative and management role, I was one of the go-to members qualified to provide training. I took it upon myself to get involved with the Associations of Certified Fraud Examiners (ACFE) and Certified Anti–Money Laundering Specialists (ACAMS), and even obtained their certifications, which gave me somewhat of a leg up. I was even invited to speak at several of the associations' events.

A group of us provided over a week of training in Jamaica to the Jamaica Constabulary Force. The force provided a driver to take us between the hotel and the training centre. Since the Jamaican driver, a full constable, had to wait for us anyway, he asked if he could take the training with us, which we of course agreed to. The young officer turned out to be extremely bright and showed a tremendous aptitude for financial investigations. The commissioner hosted a reception in our honour. I made it known to him that our driver's talents were being wasted. Two days later, when the driver picked up my colleagues, the driver unloaded on them, declaring it had taken him three years to get out of the field after being shot at, and now, due to my praise, he was being transferred back to investigations. My bad!

In Ireland, a group of us were tasked with putting together a "white paper" for the government relative to implementing proceeds-of-crime-and-money-laundering legislative and investigative requirements. One of the team was FBI agent Dennis Lormel, who had a similar career path to mine regarding undercover work. We became instant friends. Somehow, despite being taken to a bar every night, we managed to put together a fairly substantial white paper. We also learned that in Ireland, as long as there are patrons in the bar, the bar remains open!

A real highlight was travelling as a group to Colombia to provide training to the Colombian National Police, which is a part of their ministry of defence and therefore a branch of the military. As there was a million-dollar bounty at this time on any foreign law enforcement officer's head, we went in registered as business personnel. We were escorted by armed guards to the military training centre each day and in the evening, confined to a three-block radius around the hotel. Pablo Escobar's plane had been mounted on a pedestal at the training centre, a source of pride for the centre.

Our hosts offered us the opportunity to see a poppy-eradication run, and to travel to where they attempted to control FARC (the Revolutionary Armed Forces of Colombia), who claimed to be fighting for the poor. FARC's funds came from cocaine production.

We boarded the armed helicopters that served to provide security to the crop dusters that sprayed the poppy fields. It reminded me of being in a military operation—there were machine guns mounted on each side of the helicopter and each was manned by a soldier. Ironically, everyone was dressed in camouflage clothing except me. I had on a bright red windbreaker in keeping with being a Mountie. I was also sitting right by the door as we flew, so I was definitely an open target.

It is one thing to read about these things, quite another to actually take part. It affords you an entirely new perspective. The helicopters had Kevlar on the bottom to thwart the bullets of the guerrillas who protected the poppy fields below. Two runs were conducted daily in an effort to prevent the fields from being harvested. After our poppy runs, we boarded a plane and flew to the jungle, where all FARC operations took place. Definitely one for the memory book.

One other interesting investigation we took on involved GST fraud. This was before the establishment of HST. We were investigating the Hells Angels and found that they had submitted tax credits through a proliferation of shell companies pretending to export vehicles to the US. They had secured legitimate vehicle-identification numbers from various automotive lines and submitted these legitimate numbers as vehicles being shipped into the US. The volume was significant. The false invoices provided them with an avenue for rebate seeing as the government did not audit these. In the meeting we held with the CRA, I explained that the government would be money ahead if we simply did not collect GST on new vehicles. It was disappointing to me was that this did not seem to be of any major concern to them.

When 9/11 hit, I became the assistant crops (criminal operations) officer and responsible for overseeing many of the 9/11 investigations. This included Project A-O Canada, about which I could write a whole other book, but as many will know resulted in the Arar and Almalki inquiries. These were two investigations that followed the events of 9/11 after CSIS provided reports of a potential threat in the Ottawa area. The investigations called for a task force and a working cooperation with the US authorities, which included the CIA, after President W. Bush declared that the CIA and FBI would work together. Although I stand by the actions taken by the investigative team, as time has passed it has become evident that there were a number of factors involving the subjects under investigation that we were never made aware of. These hidden factors resulted in two inquiries, and in both cases, the Canadian government opted to pay out, notwithstanding the fact that our legal representatives believed we would win any civil trial.

Ironically, following 9/11, and upon my being promoted to superintendent, the commissioner directed that I be transferred to HQ to oversee the Proceeds of Crime program, when previously I'd been deemed "not political enough."

One of the first files I reviewed in my new capacity was the Airbus investigation. This investigation stemmed from allegations that the prime minister at the time, Brian Mulroney, had directly intervened in Air Canada's 1988 decision to purchase Airbus planes, as his political friends pocketed commissions and his Progressive Conservative Party grew fat on donations from Karlheinz Schreiber and campaign funds connected to the deal. This file had been under investigation for years. I conducted a detailed review, and following this, I opined that the current undercover strategy could result in creating a defence of entrapment, thus enabling the accused to show that law enforcement had entrapped them into a confession and/ or acting in an illegal capacity. The case had also been the subject of a foreign mutual legal assistant request to Switzerland that had been previously ruled as not supported by fact. For those reasons, I held the view that further actions would be seen by the courts as tainted by the previous actions. My conclusion was that this aspect of the investigation needed to be terminated. The undercover operation had not met the independence and objectivity required for a good outcome.

My decision had to be briefed up the chain of command, but I received the full support of Crime Ops Officer Antoine Couture and Commanding Officer Dawson Hovey. On April 22, 2003, the force announced the termination of the Airbus affair criminal investigation. More irony: it was the same date as the tenth anniversary of the Liberals' law-and-order platform, rooted in their supposed desire to ensure transparency and full accountability around government contracts.

Chapter Twenty-One
9/11

To this day, I vividly remember the 9/11 events. The RCMP dropped many of our criminal files and focused on the fact that another 9/11 event could occur. The investigative team on this file were all seasoned criminal investigators who were dedicated and committed to ensuring no similar event occurred in Canada. In the early days, officers worked virtually around the clock.

We relied on information from our US counterparts and our sister agency CSIS. All of us believed there was an imminent threat and that Parliament Hill was the likely target. For this reason, we convinced the government to erect blockades around the Hill.

All of the subjects of the file were provided to us by our partner agencies, surveillance, and sources. We operated with the full belief that the targets were and/or were affiliated with terrorist activities. In the investigation's early stages, I cautioned the investigators to document and record everything carefully, as I was convinced, regardless of the outcome, that we would be called to account in the future.

Our American counterparts told us that this file was briefed to the president weekly and that they had high-level concerns regarding the targets. As you know well from your vantage point, Canada was not the victim of any 9/11 attacks, and so it was upon us to fully support the US.

When search warrants were executed, we found an abundance of information that was cause for concern. Two public inquiries followed. The first commission of inquiry under the direction of Justice Dennis O'Connor focused on Maher Arar. The mandate given to Justice O'Connor in 2004 was to investigate and report on the actions of Canadian officials in relation to Maher Arar, including the following:

- the detention of Mr. Arar in the United States;
- the deportation of Mr. Arar to Syria via Jordan;
- the imprisonment and treatment of Mr. Arar in Syria;
- the return of Mr. Arar to Canada;
- any other circumstance related to Mr. Arar that Justice O'Connor considered relevant to fulfilling this mandate.

Here are further statements from the Arar inquiry report:

> On September 18, 2006, Commissioner Dennis O'Connor's public report on the events relating to Maher Arar was released. In a three-volume document, the commissioner presents the factual analysis of the case surrounding Maher Arar and submits twenty-three recommendations to the government. In accordance with his mandate, the commissioner looked into the actions of Canadian officials in relation to Maher Arar while he was detained in the United States, deported to Syria via Jordan, imprisoned in Syria, and after his return to Canada. "I am satisfied that all relevant Canadian information to the mandate have been exam-

ined," says the commissioner and "my conclusions are based on an assessment of all the evidence, regardless of whether or not it may be publicly disclosed."[20] On the issue of public disclosure, Paul Cavalluzzo, as lead commission counsel, explains: "There are portions of the public report which have been redacted because of the government's assertion of a claim of national security confidentiality (NSC). However the commissioner is of the opinion that this information should be disclosed to the public. The commissioner urges the government to refer this dispute to the federal court for an expeditious resolution so that the public might get maximum disclosure." An unredacted version of the commissioner's report has been handed to the government.

MAIN CONCLUSIONS

On Maher Arar, the commissioner comes to one important conclusion:

> I am able to say categorically that there is no evidence to indicate that Mr. Arar has committed any offence or that his activities constitute a threat to the security of Canada. The public can be confident that Canadian investigators have thoroughly and exhaustively followed all information leads available to them in connection with Mr. Arar's activities and associations. This was not a case where investigators were unable to effectively pursue their investigative goals because of a lack of resources or time constraints. On the contrary,

Canadian investigators made extensive efforts to find any information that could implicate Mr. Arar in terrorist activities. They did so over a lengthy period of time, even after Mr. Arar's case became a *cause célèbre*. The results speak for themselves: they found none.[21]

On the role of Canadian officials, taking into consideration evidence heard in public as well as in camera, the commissioner found "no evidence that Canadian officials participated or acquiesced in the American authorities' decision to detain and remove Mr. Arar to Syria . . . and there is no evidence that any Canadian authorities—RCMP, CSIS, or others—were complicit in those decisions." However, the commissioner also noted that "it is very likely that, in making the decisions to detain and remove Mr. Arar to Syria, the US authorities relied on information about Mr. Arar provided by the RCMP. Although I cannot be certain without evidence of the American authorities, the evidence strongly supports this conclusion." CSIS did not share information with the Americans at this time. The commissioner also found that both before and after Arar's detention in the US, the RCMP provided American authorities with information about Arar that was inaccurate, portrayed him in an unfair fashion, and overstated his importance to the investigation. Some of this inaccurate information had the potential to create serious consequences for Arar in light of American attitudes and practices at the time. While Arar was detained in the US, the commissioner found that officials from the Department of Foreign Affairs and International Trade took reasonable steps to provide Arar with consular services. While Arar was detained in Syria, the commissioner found that Canadian agencies relied on information about Arar (received from the Syrians) that was likely the product of torture. No adequate reliability assessment was done to determine whether this information resulted from torture. In his report, the commissioner pointed to a need for a more coherent connection between Canadian agencies when dealing with terrorism investigations; he observed a failure of communication between Canadian agencies involved in the Arar case. "There was also a lack of a single, coherent approach to efforts to obtain his release." Finally, the commissioner found that both before and after Arar's return to Canada, Canadian officials leaked confidential and sometimes inaccurate information about the case to the media for the purpose of damaging Arar's reputation or protecting their self-interest or government interests.[22]

I stated during this inquiry that we had not asked for this investigation and that we undertook it with the necessary due diligence and within our legal framework, contextualized by the backdrop of 9/11, with intelligence cautioning that we could experience a second-wave attack.

The second inquiry was headed by Justice Frank Iacobucci, who was mandated to investigate the actions of Canadian officials in relation to Abdullah Almalki, Ahmad El Maati, and Muayyed Nureddin.[23]

Both these inquiries related to the same investigation I oversaw. I can state with conviction that none of the investigators on the file supported any form of torture. We found an Al Qaeda manual that directed individuals, if arrested by foreign law enforcement in a democratic country, to claim torture. We never put the individuals on planes. They chose to do so of their own volition, to travel at that time. To this day I question why anyone would leave the safety of Canada and fly into high-risk areas, which is what led to the subjects getting arrested on foreign soil. At this time, the concept of *extraordinary rendition* was a practice none of us had ever heard of nor contemplated. In 2007, the US Senate Committee on Foreign Relations stated:

> Rendition is the practice of detaining a terrorist
> operative in a foreign country and transferring him
> or her to the United States or to another foreign
> country. It has proved to be an effective way to take
> terrorists off the street and collect, on occasion,
> some valuable information.[24]

Our investigation relied heavily on CSIS information. We worked this case using the rule of law and following all necessary court requirements for wiretaps and the execution of search warrants. The outlier was our daily correspondence with our US counterparts, which included CIA operatives, something I never would have foreseen for a Canadian criminal investigation.

With respect to Arar, a payment of ten million dollars was made following the inquiry and without a civil trial. In the second case, we began working with justice lawyers and were mounting a strong defence to demonstrate we had followed the rule of law and that the measures we used were primarily due to the suspicious activities of the accused. The government paid out to Arar, Ahmad El Maati, and Mohamad Kamal Elzahabi without the benefit of the civil process. Our legal representatives felt we had a legitimate case and that the chance of any civil action being favourable to those individuals was minimal.

Although I won't guess why this decision was taken, I firmly believe there was more to this story than the investigative team was ever privy to. My expertise would indicate there were deals cut early on with the individuals by an organization (or organizations) who remained anonymous. It is disheartening that the force and our government were willing to throw investigators under the bus.

The US government's use of rendition has been controversial, to say the least. Foreign governments have criticized this practice because it "operates outside the rule of law and has allegedly been used to transfer suspects to countries that torture or mistreat them, or to seek extraterritorial prisons in countries where we have listed the countries as abusing the human rights of their fellow citizens."[25]

It was not until well after the investigation concluded and during preparation for the hearings that this criticism came to light. I also came to the realization that neither our American counterparts nor CSIS had been totally up front with us. This caused a number of issues, and I would guess also contributed to the hearing outcomes.

My first day of testimony for the hearings occurred while I was chief of police. I had learned the day before, that all of the team, including myself, had been served with what they term "section 13 notices," which under the inquiry act is given by the inquiry commissioner to indicate he may find the person(s) named as having been involved in wrongdoing. My opening statement was to emphasize to the hearing commissioner that I was in charge and that any actions taken by the team were done with my tacit approval. This resulted in the negation of all other notices except for mine and that of the investigative lead, Mike Cabana.

During the hearings it also became abundantly clear that the majority of the officers above me had selective memory, with the exception of OIC Criminal Operations Antoine Couture. Senior HQ command, including the commissioner, claimed that they were not kept current, when in fact we submitted daily updates. Some even tried to paint the team as being somewhat "keystone," which is so typical of senior RCMP and many HQ officers who have not been in the trenches and will not demand an ethical response to the organization's problems. Far too many officers fail to take full responsibility for their actions and will instead play politics and feign ignorance of facts to throw the blame down to the lower ranks.

I offered to appear with Commissioner Zaccardelli in September 2006 when he was summoned to the House of Commons to discuss Project A-O Canada (at the end of which, having appeared alone to represent us, he apologized for the investigation). Project O was an anti-terrorism investigation created in response to the 9/11 attacks. Project A-O was the Ottawa subdivision of the investigation. As one of the most knowledgeable investigators on the file, I believe it was a fatal mistake for the commissioner to show up solo, unless he was concerned about the real fact that ongoing status reports continually flowed to HQ and that without a doubt, both he and Deputy Commissioner Gary Loeppky would have received ongoing updates from my team throughout the unfolding of Project A-O Canada. On top of this, the information we acted on required pursual. Although it was accepted that torture had occurred, this had not been condoned by the investigative team. I would opine the information obtained during the investigation fully supported the investigative process. This was a time when speaking truth to power was required.

Upon transferring to Headquarters as the national director of the Proceeds of Crime program, I was informed that I would be reporting to the assistant commissioner, but this again was a half truth, as instead they transferred a chief superintendent over from the financial-crime program. The assistant commissioner had been my boss in the division before, and although I had respect for him, he had not fully supported me following my role as representative for the inspectors and superintendents, or my taking on the Miller operation. This event again highlighted for me that the RCMP had not progressed into a modern police force. Our old paramilitary ways continued to rule the day.

Chapter Twenty-Two

LEAVING THE FORCE

Shortly after I moved to my new position as director of Proceeds of Crime in Headquarters, the commissioner's office asked me to prepare a report that would justify purchasing a twin-engine Pilatus. I asked whether the fuel capacity would permit flying directly from Toronto to the Caribbean, where it was necessary to operate due to the transhipment of drugs. When it was revealed that its range would not permit this type of travel and that it was to be used by senior command, I expressed that as I had already written a report that had eliminated Commissioner Murray's jet, there was no way I could now reverse what was a sound position based on treasury-board guidelines. At this, the commissioner's executive informed me that the report was mandatory, and that I was to write it. I said I would comply upon written direction from Commissioner Zaccardelli. I knew this was a career-ending move—I believed Zaccardelli expected unquestioning loyalty, and disobeying the directive to justify this purchase would result in my being deemed "not promotable"—but integrity is important. I was not about to betray my moral compass. I would not pander to the whims of senior leaders and set aside my beliefs to put forth a position contrary to what I'd written in a previous study.

I determined that amongst all of the IPOC units, we were carrying a 35 percent vacancy rate, a contributor to the sliding rate of our success. Our seizure and prosecution rates had dropped significantly. Following consultation with each one of the units, I drafted a report that detailed the financial and human-resource increases that would be required if the RCMP was to be in a position to fulfill their mandate and effectively pursue money-laundering and proceeds-of-crime investigations. The full complement of investigators Canada-wide was noted as 350 positions, but we were sitting around 225. We needed to either permit over-ranking or create a new rank model for federal investigators, since part of the vacancy problem arose from investigators winning promotions in other areas of the force.

There was a systemic problem with the RCMP's approach to their federal policing responsibilities.

The force, a paramilitary organization, is founded on contract policing, even though its mandate is federal policing. The vast majority of members and eventual senior leaders come from contract policing. On top of this, commanding officers have to juggle two masters—the provincial Attorney General's mandate and the federal mandate—and the provincial directives usually win the day. At this point in my career, I realized that nothing would change and that my days were numbered.

I agreed to be interviewed by Julien Sher, who was in the process of writing his book *The Road to Hell: How the Biker Gangs Are Conquering Canada*, co-authored by William Marsden, which focuses on the outlaw motorcycle gangs (referring to the Outlaws Motorcycle Club, the Hells Angels, and the various puppet clubs). Here's the quote I provided for the book:

In the seventies they were street thugs. We have watched them grow into multinational organizations. My own opinion is that the bikers are North American law enforcement's collective failure.

When we discussed the money-laundering situation that existed in 2002, I told Sher, "For years we were one of the weak links in the chain. We just didn't have the systems in place." Now, more than twenty years later, we have even become weaker. We have earned the reputation as "the Maytag of the North," a haven for transnational organized crime. After several months, I remembered the two pieces of advice given to me by Dick Dickens and Rod Stamler. One, if you don't like what you see on your list about HQ, it's time to leave, and two, to always leave on a high note. The promotion-hungry atmosphere back in HQ was intolerable to me. I saw that the only concern of many newly commissioned officers was getting their next promotion rather than attending to the task at hand. One incident drove this home for me. I was at a luncheon meeting where Commissioner Zaccardelli was going to be speaking. Loeppky introduced the commissioner, which was odd in and of itself, seeing as all of us were officers and knew the commissioner well. Loeppky told us that every time he heard the commissioner speak, the hair stood up on the back of his neck. This type of ridiculous sycophantic behaviour has never sat well with me. My belief was that we were obligated to support the office, but that the person occupying it had to *earn* our respect. Comments about being on his train or getting off never seemed to bolster team efforts. If you shared your opinion on something and it was in conflict with your superior then you were seen as not being a team player, whereas in my philosophy, if everyone agrees with me, then we do not need everyone.

The other cue that it was time to leave was that I was fighting to keep expert specialized police officers within the Proceeds of Crime units, arguing with senior managers, and requesting we over-rank so that expertise could remain within the units. The largest deployment is within contracts, meanwhile federal policing is never given its due. An erosion of expertise is the result. Far too many officers lacked the understanding and experience necessary to ensure the existence of highly effective and efficient federal policing units, and those who *were* skilled enough were more concerned about their next promotion.

The lack of focus on federal roles was evident in the case of Tom Pickard, an RCMP member in Alberta. Tom had been permitted to travel to foreign jurisdictions to help in our foreign-training efforts due to the expertise he'd gained while working in the Edmonton unit. The foreign exposure increased his knowledge and put him on a path to become one of few high-level proceeds-and-money-laundering investigators. As so often happened, he was offered a position back in uniform. I went to great efforts to intervene and even spoke to Don McDermott, a commanding officer I knew well and had great respect for. But uniform won the day, as the senior executives still did not endorse keeping qualified RCMP members within their areas of expertise. Meanwhile, outside of policing, you don't see surgeons moving into accounting roles.

Even though we already had a high vacancy rate, the commissioner decided to form a new team: Integrated Market Enforcement. Dr. Peter German, who oversaw both the proceeds and commercial-crime units, offered promotional-level positions to highly skilled officers in both these areas, resulting in further erosion. It seemed futile to fight for what should have been fully endorsed by all levels of the RCMP. Keeping all units staffed and specialized was not a priority. My concerns had been dismissed for far too long. I decided my time in the force was coming to an end.

George Wool, a former RCMP commercial-crime investigator who practised law in Surrey, BC, summed it up best in 2001. He said it is this typical kind of unhealthy relationship between the police and the government that convinced him to leave the federal force after twenty-one years. He believes the former commissioner's remarks—which sound like something a politician would say to try to ensure re-election—reveal that the line between policing and politics has been unacceptably blurred in Canada, opening the door for misuse of government and/or police powers. In a unit set up by my mentor Rod Stamler, Wool was one of the original commercial-crime investigators. In a 2001 *Windspeaker* newspaper article, Paul Barnsley writes that Stamler is "an old-school police officer who quit the RCMP in disgust when the Mulroney government changed the way the police interact with the government after several cabinet ministers were investigated and charged." In that same article, Wool is quoted speaking on the questionable relationship of the RCMP and the government.

> There was an old saying, back in the sixties. Judges used to remind police officers that 'you are the eyes and ears of the court.' You're not the eyes and ears of the media; you're not the eyes and ears of the politicians. The politicians should have no more standing in the police office than the lowly drug addict or drunk. What they've done is they've politicized the RCMP to the point where an agency like Indian Affairs can say, 'Here, you investigate such and such a band.' I find it somewhat corrupt to hear investigations being directed against Native bands in New Brunswick or Nova Scotia. That's targeting. Yet the RCMP here in British Columbia does absolutely nothing about the Hells Angels or these Asian gangs. They're not targeted the same way. And they're criminal organizations.[26]

When I was head-hunted for a chief's position in January 2003, I attempted to have a discussion with Deputy Commissioner Garry Loeppky. On each occasion, his executive assistant said he was too busy to see me. After trying for three weeks, I decided to leave, and that was when both Garry Loeppky and Zack Zaccardelli found the time to see me. But at this juncture, it was too late for any meaningful discussion. Their delay confirmed that my decision was in the best interest of my family and my health.

As I've noted many times, at no time was I ever afforded any support relative to potential mental health issues and how work-related events affected my family. I fully accept that I lived in a time in the history of policing when it was not considered professional to show any weakness. This was not malicious on anyone's part—it was simply due to the times we were in during this policing era. But this does not condone the lack of professional support. When people stay silent, avoid reality, and refuse to acknowledge the truths that are right in front of them, transformation for the better cannot occur.

The culture of the force needs a major overhaul. That much is urgently apparent. Senior leaders continue to fail the organization, their rank and file, and society. Part of the problem stems from the RCMP trying to be all things to all people. The complexities law enforcement faces today demand focused teams—teams who aren't pulled in all directions.

Far too many members were in situations like mine and were left to their own devices. In our day, it is widely documented that people often rely on drinking and drugs to cope. Addiction harms officers and impacts their families, too. The threats on my life had a profound impact on me, the depth of which I did not accept until long after leaving the force, and only after my youngest daughter, who now works in the mental health field, pointed it out in real terms. I now realize I have suffered from PTSD for years. My stress disorder absolutely influenced how I approached certain aspects of my career. It took a toll. I used humour and buried myself in my work to compensate. It is hard to admit, but honesty is a great first step.

Despite the negative factors I witnessed in the force, I would repeat my career in a heartbeat—hopefully as a somewhat smarter man, yet with the same operational commitment. The force's areas of weakness have now mushroomed; as a result, the force has little to no integrity within its most senior ranks. Well-intentioned members are not afforded the opportunity to become experts in a given area. This is a failing of senior leaders and the government.

Chapter Twenty-Three

POST-RCMP

After leaving the RCMP, I became the chief of police of Cobourg. It was a role I held for about four years. Although I was hired to amalgamate policing in Northumberland County, once I was in the position, I found out that the amalgamation was desired by Cobourg and only Cobourg—the matter had not been discussed with the surrounding municipalities. Through the board chair, Alan Robinson (with whom I became close friends), I learned Mayor Peter Delanty had been opposed to my hiring, allegedly stating I would never do as I was told. Well, damn, he was right!

I joked that the Hatfields and McCoys were alive and well—Port Hope and Cobourg were like archenemies. Despite the study I conducted that revealed there were substantial financial savings to be had by amalgamating the two police services, they deemed working together to be out of the question.

In my first year as chief, Officer Christopher Garrett was murdered while taking a fake robbery call. This was one of the hardest times in my policing career. Only a chief can fully understand this pressure; the organization and the community all had their eyes on how I would manage the tragedy. In the short time I had been in

Cobourg, I had gotten to know Chris as an extremely capable officer, focused on being hands on more so than aiming for a supervisory or management role. As a small department, the devastation of his murder tore the heart and soul out of us, and out of the town.

In my time in Cobourg, I was able to get the police building refurbished, though this was not initially welcomed. Spending money on police was not appreciated by the council, many of whom could be described as the "old guard" of the town. The renovation transpired with a degree of seriousness after I had the Ministry of Labour conduct an audit, which led to an order being issued against myself, the Police Services Board, and the town administrator. The refurbishment truly should not have required this strategy, but a chief is accountable for ensuring that police standards are met. Politics cannot rule the day.

Following the station's renovations, I focused on the courts and the deplorable state of the cells, which put both our special constables and the inmates at risk. With the help once again of the Ministry of Labour, we reached some agreements, including time-lines to move the court facilities and to have new safe cell facilities attached to the court building. This pitted me against many on the town council and a few board members aligned with council.

When I alerted the board and the council to a pending drug problem, as heroin was being noted on the street, the problem was dismissed. Both groups felt I was overreacting. I am not saying we could have curtailed what's become prevalent today, but perhaps if we had taken this seriously, we could have at least shut down some of the traffickers. Today, the situation is virtually out of control, and addicts abound on the streets of Cobourg.

Although I made some mistakes, I am proud to say I was able to align the standards with provincial expectations. I also introduced to Cobourg the ability to process criminal-record checks, a massive revenue generator that has grown the Cobourg Police's annual gross revenue from a few hundred thousand dollars to around four million today.[27] My role as chief also showed me, as someone who'd spent the majority of his career in a federal policing role, that uniform and federal requirements are substantially different, mandating different skills and different management styles.

I remained committed to fighting organized crime. Even during my time in Cobourg, I agreed to participate as an expert witness in an organized-crime trial in Montreal. This was a textbook case in that it illustrated just how organized crime operates and the way these groups work together. Internationally, the case revealed transshipment routes for cocaine and money laundering, involving an international bank established in Cambodia. The case also showed the evolution of a drug trafficker. One man in particular. From a small street trafficker to an international importer dealing with some of the highest levels of organized crime, Daniel Muir had an extensive record. That record began in 1998 when he received an eighteen-month sentence for conspiracy to traffic 225 grams of cocaine and 3,944 grams of cannabis resin. In 1992, he received a four-month sentence and a twenty-thousand-dollar fine for conspiracy to traffic in one kilogram of cocaine. Also in 1992, he received a six-year sentence for conspiracy to traffic six kilos of cocaine and eight kilos of cannabis resin. In 1997 his parole was revoked for conspiracy to import cannabis resin.

In 2002 the US Drug Enforcement Administration established that in 2000, 1,200 kilos of intercepted cocaine were suspected of being destined for Muir. In the same year, a further seizure of eight hundred kilos from what was believed to be a 1,400-kilogram shipment was again suspected of being arranged for Muir. The DEA had intelligence involving another 12,000-kilogram shipment of cocaine destined for Muir later that year as well. In 2003, Muir and his counterparts received eight hundred kilos of cocaine, some of which was water-damaged, so another 150 kilograms were ordered. Between 2003 and 2004, intelligence revealed that $1.3 million

CHAPTER TWENTY-THREE

US were deposited in Costa Rica, allegedly for the 2003 shipment of cocaine.

Trial testimony during the preliminary hearing revealed that Muir had large sums of cash available to him at all times, and that he paid cash for all his business and private expenses. Amounts in the tens of thousands of dollars. Muir went to great lengths to conceal his property ownership, relying on friends, female companions, and his money launderers, M. Sy Veng Chun and Mme Leng Ky Lech (whom Muir referred to as "*la petite madame chinoise*").[28] Chun and Lech were the owners of two businesses running from the same location: A&A Services Monétaires Inc. and Peng Heng Or Gold Inc., a money exchange in Montreal that evidence proved was exchanging drug money and moving funds offshore.

In November 2006, Sergeant Benoît Roy of the RCMP reached out to me seeking my support to review a case they had concluded and, if possible, to provide an expert affidavit. I eagerly took on the challenge. The facts resembled the plot of a Hollywood movie.

Lech and Chun accommodated drug traffickers who needed money exchanged from US dollars to Canadian dollars and vice versa. We discovered that Chun and Lech had established a bank in Cambodia. They also worked for many Asian-based clothing businesses in Montreal that were in fact fronts to attempt to legitimize criminal profits.

We gathered evidence through the testimony of many of Lech and Chun's clients. In one case, a Richard Beauregard testified that he managed the money for trafficker Marc-Andre Cusson, and that he'd exchanged approximately ten million dollars through Lech and Chun. Chun had offered him gold bars and the option to move money to their alleged bank in Los Angeles. In another case, a Raymond Millette testified that from the winter of 2000 to August 2001, he patronized Peng Heng once or twice per week to exchange amounts earned through the sale of marijuana in the US, ranging from $150,000 to $200,000, from US to Canadian dollars.

One testimony of tremendous value, and which painted the real picture of this organization, came from a Bernard Mondou. Mondou was arrested and convicted for his involvement in an RCMP investigation known as Operation Cruiser, which was tied to a US file, Operation Busted Manatee. At the centre of the investigation was the "Cobos-Munoz" organization, described by then Attorney General John Ashcroft to be responsible for shipping multi-ton quantities of cocaine into the United States from the North Coast region of Colombia. This organization is said to have generated over $145,000,000 from their activities.[29] Mondou testified that he'd relied on Chun, and that the link to Chun was a subject known as Daniel Muir.

The testimony of Nathalie Jean, Muir's common-law spouse, confirmed Muir was a major cocaine importer and trafficker. She had knowledge that Muir kept his money in cash, unless he was moving through Chun. According to Jean, Muir socialized with Frank Cotroni, which would justify his ability to bring large amounts of cocaine into Montreal.

During the trial, it would emerge that Bernard Mondou had helped Muir smuggle cocaine from Colombia into the United States, and that a Montreal police officer named Pierre Goulet, a childhood friend of Mondou's, brought Muir's money from Montreal into the US for Mondou.

Muir and Lech's deal went sour after Chun, whose primary role in the deal was to smuggle Muir's cash into Cambodia, was arrested by the RCMP at the Dorval Airport on October 12, 2002, while carrying six hundred thousand dollars in a suitcase. He'd been about to depart to Cambodia.

On one occasion, Muir purchased a condo in Mexico and Chun handled the down payment. Through Jean, information surfaced that Muir had invested over one hundred million dollars in Chun's bank in Cambodia and that he likely had another sixty million dollars available. According to Jean, there'd been a falling out with

Chun after she refused to continue paying the eighty grand monthly interest on the deposit in Cambodia.

Daniel Muir and Nathalie divorced. Karine Descoteaux, Muir's subsequent common-law spouse, confirmed much of Jean's testimony. Testimony was also gathered from Suzanne Pépin, an alleged clairvoyant whose instincts Muir and Jean had trusted enough to request that she size up Lech and Chun before Muir would agree to hand over millions of his money for them to launder. Lech and Chun planned to use the money to start their own bank in their native Cambodia.

According to Pépin, Muir's life was completely steered by his emotions. Pépin testified that Muir should not go through with the deal, but he ignored her advice and over the course of about four years, gave the couple an estimated hundred million dollars to be laundered. Pépin testified that she witnessed Lech retrieve boxes of suspected cash from Muir's residence on multiple occasions. Muir had placed his residential purchases in close associates' names, including Lech's.

I find it particularly interesting that Muir became transfixed by the clairvoyant, Pépin, and by a monk introduced to him by Chun and Lech. He even created an altar in his home and pressured the monk to spend time with him. Muir's paranoia may have been related to his cocaine usage.

Four years after his initial meeting with Chun and Lech, Muir was murdered on the streets of Montreal. This was not unheard of for a high-level trafficker, but what *was* unique is the fact that he was killed in a manner that I would describe as a triad-style killing. On February 3, 2004, Muir had just left Club Wanda's strip club downtown when he was killed by two men, one carrying an axe, the other a knife. Whether this occurred as a result of the pressure he was placing on Chun and Lech, or from the loss of his last shipment, we simply don't know.[30] Daniel Muir was forty-one when he was killed. The murder has never been solved.

POST-POLICING: EXPERTISE DEMANDS
ONGOING TRAINING

Early on in my policing career I recognized the value of certification organizations. I became an early adopter of the Association of Certified Fraud Examiners and was fortunate to get to know the founders. After returning from Hong Kong, I became actively engaged with the Association of Certified Anti–Money Laundering Specialists and was fortunate enough to be offered a seat on the advisory board thanks to the founder, Charles Intriago. Through this I was given the opportunity to engage with some of the most talented AML specialists around the world, like former New York state trooper Kevin Sullivan; former IRS agent Mike McDonald (who'd worked in Miami during the massive cocaine insurgence by the cartels); former customs agent and deputy director of the Financial Crimes Enforcement Network (FinCEN)—the US equivalent to the Financial Transactions and Reports Analysis Centre of Canada (FINTRAC)—Connie Fenchel; former FBI special agent Dennis Lormel; and banking experts Jim Richards, Dan Soto, Barry Koch, and John Byrne. And countless others, far too many to name. Additionally, I was the founder of three Canadian AML chapters in Toronto, Vancouver, and Montreal. The chapters created an opportunity for anti–money laundering professionals to collaborate and for training to be provided by recognized experts in their subject matter. It also provided me with an enhanced understanding of how the entire financial community can be taken advantage of by money launderers.

In late 2014, I became involved with the newest association, the Association of Certified Financial Crime Specialists, which fell in under BARBRI (a US company that provides legal training to graduates in preparation for the bar exams) and Chairman Stephen Fredette. I worked under contract with the association during this difficult time in its evolution. As the new group on the block, the association was not well-known and was failing to garner the critical mass necessary to be viable. That being said, its certification was tremendously valuable and highly recognized within the world of fraud fighters and accountants. Although I failed to achieve all my goals during my tenure, I was able to use my network and contacts to raise the association's profile and make concrete recommendations for revamping the training. The strategic plan detailing the need for strong chapters has now taken root, which should serve the financial-crime community well for years to come.

Forming my own consulting company definitely took a leap of faith. I wanted to maintain engagement with the financial sector, assist in thwarting financial crime, and on the investigative side, use my expertise to help corporations with their investigative needs. My initial objective was to create an organization that would be recognized as the premier firm in Canada for anti–money laundering and corporate investigation. My problem was that when I started in 2009, my competitive advantage was that all my clients received personal one-on-one service with me, rather than being assigned to less experienced individuals. This approach helped the company thrive; however, all the work generated directly involved me. Despite the company's success, I realized that its growth was unsustainable and resigned myself to enjoying the smaller-scale triumphs of my personal endeavours—I decided to keep the company small.

As the sole decision-maker, I was able to keep my rates highly competitive due to very low overhead. The downside was that it put my workaholic personality into high gear, using work to mask my PTSD.

In 2018, following a move back to Ottawa, I agreed to sell my consulting client list to the AML Shop, a group I had collaborated with for many years. I'd injured myself during the move and recognized that I needed a break and wouldn't be able to service my clients for an extended period. I maintained the investigative side of the business until 2022, at which point I sold to Lodestar Security Solutions in Ottawa, a company I had partnered with for a few years.

You might think that after working for this many years, I would be heading toward retirement. And yes, it *was* on the radar.

In 2021, I was asked to be on the board of directors of a proposed bank in Barbados. James Lau, the previous founder of Jameson MTFX and later Jameson Bank, was heading a group to obtain a bank licence. I agreed and contributed to initial discussions with the Barbados prime minister and the governor of the banks. In one of these meetings, the president of VersaBank, David Taylor, heard me speak and arranged to meet with me separately, resulting in an offer to become the chief AML officer. I was initially less than enthusiastic, but I did agree to travel to London, Ontario, to speak with VersaBank's compliance team and senior leaders.

Agreeing to become a chief AML officer brought me full circle relative to having a profound and comprehensive understanding of all the gaps that exist within Canada's anti–money launder-ing regime. VersaBank, at the time of writing, is in the process of obtaining a US bank licence, having purchased Stearns Bank's Holdingford branch in Minnesota, which will expand my portfolio to include the Bank Secrecy Act requirements. Having now worked in the bank since March 2022, I can confidently say that the presi-dent is one of the better senior executives I've had the opportunity to work with in my forty-nine years of a focus on financial crime and transnational organized crime.

As a chief anti–money laundering officer, I am afforded the opportunity to sit on Canadian Bankers Association commit-tees, broadening my understanding of some of the concerns of our financial institutions, which, perhaps naïvely, many former law-enforcement officers are not fully aware of. It's also allowed for my ongoing interaction with FINTRAC, an organization I've witnessed grow from the ground floor and have liaised with since its beginning.

I have been honoured to know some prolific investigative jour-nalists who have written on many of the subjects I've explored in this book. I have been cited in a number of published works written by individuals such as Julien Sher, Terry Gould, and Paul Palango, and there are others I consider friends and positive influencers, like Victor Malarek, Fabian Dawson, Declan Hill, and most recently Sam Cooper. I am sure many law-enforcement officers and politicians would disagree with me, but I believe we need a vibrant and effective press. It serves to keep everyone honest, even if the report is painful to read.

Part Seven

WHAT DO WE DO?

Chapter Twenty-Four

RECOMMENDATIONS

I hope that the preceding chapters and the details of my career have provided an overview of the evolution of the RCMP since the seventies—a time before computers, when police and criminals played on a level field. As technology thrived, the extensive resources of organized crime evolved faster than those of law enforcement, who were limited by shrinking budgets and an inability to pivot to prioritize the need for expert investigators and laws commensurate with the evolution of criminal activity.

After testifying before the Cullen Commission, collaborating on a book spearheaded by Jamie Ferrill and Dr. Christian Leuprecht entitled *Dirty Money: Financial Crime in Canada* (published in 2023 by McGill-Queen's University Press), and most recently writing a submission to the Department of Finance on the five-year review of the Proceeds of Crime (Money Laundering) and Terrorist Financing Act, I have had the opportunity to reflect and to gather my thoughts on what is needed in Canada. To overcome certain weaknesses in the RCMP and in our ability to combat organized crime, I offer the following recommendations.

UNDER COVER

THE NEED FOR A CULTURE CHANGE WITHIN THE RCMP: A COMPLETE REVAMPING

Much has been written over the last decade on this subject. The media has exposed us to civil suit after civil suit dealing with multiple RCMP misdeeds stemming from a clear lack of cultural awareness. It has been disheartening to see what can only be described as the decline of the RCMP. This is not a slam against the many dedicated young members, but of current and former senior management who seem to be continuously embroiled in controversy. It is time that the force report to an independent oversight board, not to the serving party. This independent body should be made up of community leaders, judges, academics, and individuals in the legal community. Independence is an absolute must. Such a change may help reduce the current level of politicization.

Changing the current culture in the RCMP with its multiple competing mandates is virtually impossible. Making a change will require a fundamental structural shift; I recommend relinquishing contract policing. The RCMP, first and foremost, is a federal police service who has taken on uniform policing in all provinces except Ontario and Quebec. Prior to the contemporary complexities imposed by organized crime, terrorism, cybercrime, and financial crime, the RCMP used to be able to meet the demands of its multiple duties in an admirable way. Today, however, the reality is that the RCMP cannot meet all of its demands. As a result, Canada's ability to tackle transnational organized crime, complex financial investigations, terrorism, and other criminal issues has been eroded to a point that should cause everyone concern. About ten years ago, I concluded that with the the growing sophistication of financial crime and organized crime, Canada would need to rethink the RCMP. It is now time for an awakening. Canadians are paying a high price for inaction, and organized crime is only getting wealthier and more powerful.

Although I know many RCMP officers were extremely disappointed in the position taken on the Surrey policing issue, wherein the Government of BC directed Surrey County Council to move forward with the formation of a municipal force, it was the right decision. I firmly believe that members of the RCMP are capable of carrying out effective and efficient contract duties; however, the organization as a whole must re-evaluate its future. Contract policing is exactly that: a contract. Federal and protective policing are central to the Royal Canadian Mounted Police's function. To be effective and efficient, federal and protective policing must be of primary concern, rather than play second fiddle to the provincial and municipal contracts.

THE NEED FOR A COMPREHENSIVE REVIEW OF OUR LEGISLATION

Canada's Charter of Rights has resulted in some court decisions that make tackling organized crime and complex financial investigations very difficult. We need to find a balanced and measured approach to dealing with the ramifications of the 1991 Stinchcombe decision, in which "the Crown has a legal duty to disclose all relevant information to the defence"[31] and the Jordan decision of the Supreme Court of Canada, which rejected the framework traditionally used to determine whether an accused has been tried within a reasonable time under section 11(b) of the Canadian Charter of Rights and Freedoms. That framework has been replaced with a ceiling of eighteen months between the charges and the trial in a provincial court without preliminary inquiry, or thirty months in other cases.[32] The Stinchcombe decision states:

> The fruits of the investigation which are in its possession are not the property of the Crown for

use in securing a conviction but the property of the public to be used to ensure that justice is done.[33]

Never in the history of common law has a decision (in this case, two decisions) so affected our ability to seek to obtain convictions when confronted with organized crime and transnational organized-crime cases. The burden of disclosure, as well as foreign authorities' reluctance to cooperate due to the "full and frank disclosure" requirements, have contributed greatly to what many police leaders now refer to as *the trial of the investigation, and not the accused.*

A trial today enables every aspect of the investigation to be placed under a microscope, including all investigative actions. In some cases, even officers' personnel files have been demanded in order to show any past shortcomings. When you are dealing, in financial-crime case, with thousands of documents and numerous search warrants, errors are bound to occur—there must be a balance between actual justice and concerns about whether or not it is being brought into disrepute.

I find it extremely difficult to comprehend how we can simply discharge an accused involved in rape, murders, and other serious criminal activity due to the violation of their right to a speedy trial. How can the entire justice system look a victim in the eye and, in good conscience, say that the system is doing a good job? I would submit that in such cases, "justice is bringing itself into disrepute." I feel that if such an event happened to a sitting judge's family, or a minister's, different action would be taken.

I hope that legal scholars may yet draft legislation to offset the impact of the Jordan and Stinchcombe decisions in the cases of organized crime and serious violent crimes. The justice system owes society the ability to deal with major criminals who terrorize our society for their benefit.

We need to consider establishing some new laws to make it easier to combat organized crime, as these criminals do not play by the rules. Certain legal tools are needed to be able to investigate and prosecute them. If we want to be effective through enforcement, new legislation, such as a wire-fraud statute, is worth looking into. The US has defined wire fraud as "a crime in which a person schemes to defraud or obtain money using electronic communications or an interstate communications facility."[34] In the United States, the statute of limitations to bring a wire-fraud charge is five years, unless the wire fraud targeted a financial institution, in which case the statute of limitations is doubled to ten years. Implementing a similar practice here in Canada would help us prosecute criminal organizations moving criminally derived money by electronic means.

Another element Canada should consider implementing is a Racketeer Influenced and Corrupt Organizations (RICO) statute similar to the United States'. Their statute covers "any act of bribery, counterfeiting, theft, embezzlement, fraud, dealing in obscene matter, obstruction of justice, slavery, racketeering, gambling, money laundering, commission of murder-for-hire, and many other offences covered under Title 18 of the federal criminal code."[35] I realize an argument could be made that many provinces have civil forfeiture provisions, so the RICO statute may not be necessary for our country, but I would argue that Canada needs strong federal tools in additional to the provincial measures, since transnational organized-crime groups do not recognize borders, whether provincial or international.

Legislative amendments to the Proceeds of Crime (Money Laundering) and Terrorist Financing Act were intended to require lawyers to report suspicious activities and large cash transactions. In my affidavit I argued that corrupt people use financial techniques to hide their proceeds of crime, and it is these influential professionals who are used unwittingly to ensure effective money laundering, which, in my view, requires the use of professionals like lawyers to place illegally obtained proceeds beyond the reach of law enforcement by moving the bulk cash through the financial system. These professionals act as the vehicle to move money from a cash-based system into a business-based system. I argued that lawyers are used to facilitate the creation of corporate vehicles, the purchase and sale of property, the bestowal of financial and tax advice, introductions to financial institutions, and financial transactions.

Lastly, I took the position that the exemption sought by lawyers would seriously impair the legitimate steps taken by the government to investigate and prosecute money launderers. This is a position I steadfastly stand behind today, even though the Supreme Court sided with the law societies—which means that today, lawyers are not required to report as it would interfere with solicitor-client privilege.[36] Had they lost their challenge, the lawyers would have had to report large cash transactions of ten thousand dollars or more, as well as document and identify all clients and report suspicious transactions. The decision not to require such reporting was, in my view, self-serving. It does not recognize reality. The fact is that money laundering demands the use of professionals.

In 1959, President John F. Kennedy gave a speech at a district attorneys' convention. Some of the statements he made then ring true today:

> I am not talking about juvenile delinquency or petty thievery. I am talking about the real heart of the matter: the growing power of the organized underworld—the criminal syndicates which have achieved control over an increasing number of legitimate business enterprises.
>
> Frequently, the nature of a legitimate business serves to assist these illicit operations. Narcotics smugglers, posing as importers, conceal drugs in barrels of olive oil or in the heart of huge cheeses. Those posing as garment manufacturers have

access to acetic anhydride, which is used to treat rayon but can also be used to convert raw opium into a morphine base for heroin. Those engaged in trucking operations have access to the waterfront, to facilitate their smuggling.

Other legitimate businesses—such as jukeboxes, laundries, and bars, make available large amounts of coin and cash which cannot be traced. Consequently it is not surprising that, of the fifty-eight known hoodlums in attendance at the famous Apalachin, New York, meeting in November of 1957, nine had been in the coin-operated machine business; sixteen were involved in garment manufacturing or trucking; ten owned grocery stores or markets; seventeen owned taverns or restaurants; eleven were in the olive oil–cheese importing or exporting business; nine were in the construction business; and others were involved in automotive agencies, coal companies, entertainment, funeral homes, ownership of horses and racetracks, linen and laundry enterprises, trucking, waterfront activities and bakeries, and one was a conductor of a dance band. Fifty of these men, as you no doubt know, had criminal records. But many of them were not ordinary criminals. They have surrounded themselves with respectability—with lawyers and accountants and political connections. They have their own elaborate organizations, their own systems of discipline and sanctions—their own code of rules and their own hired executioners. They are hard to find, hard to accuse, and very hard to convict.[37]

Our weak laws and our disorganized and moderately funded law enforcement are no match for transnational organized-crime groups. Canada has been ineffective in tackling Italian-based organized crime for decades, and as such, the second and third generations have sufficient wealth to enter into quasi-legitimate businesses, thereby being far more effective and efficient in any illegal operations undertaken. Asian-based organized crime continues to operate with virtual impunity. Recent news articles have highlighted just how brazen they have become.

In 2003, just prior to leaving the force, I was asked to prepare affidavits on two matters: the civil forfeiture Charter challenge in Ontario, and the Federation of Law Societies of Canada's challenge of the extension of the proceeds-of-crime provisions that imposed reporting obligations on lawyers. The Chatterjee case was spearheaded by Jeffrey Simser from the Ontario civil forfeiture unit. The case was simple and clean and had all the necessary facts to justify an opinion that the monies found were, "on a balance of probabilities," the fruits of drug trafficking. This made its way to the Supreme Court, who subsequently upheld the province's right to use civil forfeiture. This was a huge win for provincial governments in their fight against organized crime, which set the stage for other provinces to enact similar forfeiture legislation.

Since leaving policing, I have become a spokesperson, through national media, for the issues I've spoken about in this book. I've openly agreed to do interviews in the hopes of highlighting the deficiencies that exist in Canada. I also continue to speak at both national and international conferences with one goal: getting out the message that globally organized crime is making a laughingstock of our national and international efforts to combat fraud, money laundering, cybercrime, and other criminal activities.

Having studied and focused on money laundering, it is disheartening to reflect on current events. Russian oligarchs freely launder money they pilfer from the Russian Federation in the UK,

New York, Saudi Arabia, and Dubai. Asian criminals value their friendships at the political level in United States and Canada, even while illegally acquiring numerous multimillion-dollar properties. Communities in Canada fail to ask the hard questions when alleged business owners promise to improve main streets and old heritage buildings. The fact that the criminal trades are paid in cash seems to raise no alarm bells. Why? Because the money is pouring in.

We need to recognize that corruption exists in Canada.

We should have learned from the Charbonneau Commission just how pervasive organized crime can be with respect to provincial and municipal budgets. Local politicians can be bought, leading to increased infrastructure costs and non-competitive contract bidding.

In the case of SNC-Lavalin's charges of fraud and corruption, nearly forty-eight million dollars in payments were made to Libyan government officials between 2001 and 2011.[38] This case resulted in a firestorm in the Trudeau government, but the real point is that a well-respected company acted in a manner synonymous with organized crime and yet had tentacles into government.

When Trudeau's government came to power in 2015, they promised to "refocus Canada's development assistance on helping the poorest and most vulnerable and supporting fragile states."[39] This pronouncement is best described as "political speak." It has become abundantly evident that actions taken by the Trudeau administration in 2018 against then Attorney General Jody Wilson-Raybould have been officially cited as interference in a judicial process. We witnessed how, under Trudeau's leadership, numerous actors applied pressure to have the Attorney General abandon prosecution of SNC-Lavalin.

We must not forget that SNC-Lavalin VP Normand Morin was charged with violating the Canada Elections Act for orchestrating a scheme between 2004 and 2011 to have employees donate to federal parties, which SNC would then reimburse, bypassing the legal restrictions. It was revealed that $117,803 flowed from SNC-Lavalin to federal party coffers during that period (about eight thousand dollars of that went to Conservatives, the rest to Liberals).[40]

As for the ethics commissioner's report, Mario Dion pulled no punches. He wrote a scathing report indicting the prime minister and key staff in the PMO. He felt this was a clear attempt to interfere and therefore a violation of the Conflict of Interest Act. Dion pointed out that the PMO also deliberately withheld confidential cabinet documents from the ethics commission.

I appeared on *Power & Politics* with journalist Robert Fife to discuss the situation regarding Senator Mike Duffy. Although he was found not guilty in the courts based on poorly written Senate policies, I am sure in the court of public opinion the abuse of Canadian tax dollars did not go unnoticed. It is my position that he ought to have known right from wrong.

According to the International Monetary Fund, as much as $1.5 to $2 trillion in bribes circulate the globe annually, resulting in lost tax revenues and sustained poverty in countries desperate for economic growth. Canada has attempted to establish itself as a leader on the world stage; however, what has transpired recently epitomizes what James Cohen stated in February 2019: that Canada is "falling behind" on fighting corruption abroad. "If it's said that corruption greases the wheels of bureaucracy, then apathy and cynicism pave the path for corruption."[41]

It's time we hold our political leaders to account. What occurred in the SNC-Lavalin matter is unacceptable and if, as a society, we don't demand corruption-free practices, corruption will prevail. It's up to us.

THE NEED FOR EFFECTIVE PROTECTIONS FOR WHISTLEBLOWERS

I am currently an avid supporter of Transparency International, which, "through [the organization's] advocacy, campaigning, and research, [works] to expose the systems and networks that enable corruption to thrive."[42] I also recently agreed to be on the advisory board of Whistleblowing Canada Research Society. Like much of society, I was naïve when it came to the realization that Canada is currently at the bottom of the G20 list for having effective whistleblowing protections. Whistleblowers reveal misconduct at great personal and professional risk. Since joining the group, I have heard some heartbreaking stories. It is dreadful to realize this is happening in Canada. Each of these courageous individuals is routinely subjected to harassment, job termination, arrest, and even physical attacks for exposing wrongdoing. It is long overdue in this country that we afford whistleblowers with strong legal protections to enable them to report offences safely and freely while keeping them from retaliation.

THE NEED FOR A HIGHLY TRAINED INVESTIGATIVE BODY CAPABLE OF DEALING WITH CYBER THREATS

Experience has shown that criminal and terrorist organizations remain fluid, proactive, and take full advantage of technology. To combat this, we need a national police force composed of knowledgeable experts willing to rise to the present challenges while remaining committed to their areas of expertise. The day of the generalist police officer is no longer sustainable. The RCMP must become the FBI, DEA, and the National Security Agency of Canada.

There is a growing realization of the special importance of the national investigative and enforcement responsibilities of the RCMP. Keep in mind that when the RCMP entered its contract-policing roles, the internet didn't exist. Terrorism, organized crime, money laundering, human smuggling, and cybercrime were concepts far from Canada's shores. But just as the criminal landscape has changed, so must the RCMP.

The argument to off-load contract policing is an emotional issue that has simmered for years. Many senior RCMP leaders owe their careers to the contract-policing stream and are not anxious to see it end. As someone who started his career in contract policing, I know the value of getting a foundation there. Having been on the outside for the past two decades, however, and as someone still working in the financial community, my four-plus decades of experience have hardened my position that the current structure of the RCMP (and its way of dealing with federal resources) is not only unsustainable—but is contributing to an ever-growing organized-crime problem in Canada. A time has come for the Government of Canada to evaluate the multitude of mandates managed by the RCMP and focus on what structure will best serve Canadians, recognizing the current threat situation involving transnational organized crime, cybercrime, and financial crime.

The last Financial Action Task Force evaluation of Canada's money-laundering regime listed major issues we still need to address. The most pressing issues were identified as follows:

> a) Law-enforcement results are not commensurate with the money-laundering risk, and asset recovery is low.

> b) Financial institutions, including the six domestic systemically important banks, have a good understanding of their risks and obligations, and generally apply adequate mitigating measures. The same is not true for designated nonfinancial businesses and professions, otherwise known as "DNFBPs." Real estate firms have gradually increased their

reporting of suspicious transactions, but reporting by DNFBPs—other than by casinos—is very low.

c) Legal persons and arrangements are at a high risk of misuse, and that risk is not mitigated.

Some of the above-noted gaps have contributed to the proliferation of organized crime and transnational crime groups that rely on Canada as a safe venue. For this reason, the US Department of State designated Canada a "major money-laundering country" where foreign drug-trafficking gangs are exploiting our soft laws and feeble law enforcement.[43] The March 2019 strategy report on money laundering places Canada on a short list of countries vulnerable to significant drug money–laundering transactions, alongside Afghanistan, the British Virgin Islands, China, Colombia, and Macau.

CHINA'S RULING ELITE: THE BIGGEST TRANSNATIONAL ORGANIZED-CRIME GROUP IN THE WORLD

China must be recognized for what it is. We can no longer permit China to pursue our natural resources and interfere with our democratic processes. Far too many current and former politicians have welcomed Chinese leaders with open arms, to our country's peril. China's human-rights violations are not acceptable. Their willingness to permit precursor chemicals for the manufacture of fentanyl to flow to Mexican cartels through the triads is a flagrant violation of human rights. China's Belt and Road Initiative must be recognized for what it is—an expansion of their power throughout the free world. Our willingness to welcome Chinese international students, knowing they are obligated to report intelligence back to the regime, demonstrates our naïveté.

We need to get a full understanding, through official inquiry, of the threat that China poses, and hopefully uncover areas of risk that can be contained. The fact is, some Chinese Canadians still suffer at the hands of the regime and many businesses are forced to pay protection to the triads; this falls outside of what Canada stands for. We need a firm policy and to recognize that expertise is required to provide effective policing within our Chinese communities.

The sheer number of organized-crime cases reported for the past year by Global News investigations in British Columbia (such as the laundering of fentanyl-trafficking proceeds from China through casinos; real estate bought with the proceeds of crime; and underground banks) demonstrates that the business of organized crime is booming. A full gap analysis with a goal of devising both short-term and long-term strategies would be a big help in confronting organized crime head on. Investigations of this nature are complex and require investigators and prosecutors who have worked in this arena for several years. As there is a huge shortfall in expertise today, Canada will only be able to accomplish this kind of immediate widespread change through public and private partnerships. In the long term, with dedicated resources, and with the proviso that anyone recruited into financial-crime fighting remain in the federal enforcement arena, we will begin to see transnational crime combatted more effectively.

The government needs to accept that the legal profession is vulnerable to being used by organized crime to establish offshore trusts and shell companies, and to facilitate real estate transactions. While the bar associations have successfully argued that everything a law firm engages in has solicitor-client privilege attached to it, there needs to be a mechanism capable of reviewing all legal firms' activities. The requirement for a designated compliance officer with fiduciary responsibility for ensuring that the firm does not contribute to money laundering—an officer who could report to each law society—may be a good start.

In a recent trip to London, home of VersaBank, I spoke to a woman of second-generation Chinese descent and her husband. Through our discussions, she learned that I had worked with the police in Hong Kong. As we spoke, she elaborated on how law enforcement in Canada have no idea what occurs in the Chinese communities. She said she is well aware that many Chinese businesses in Richmond and Vancouver are forced to pay protection to the triads.

THE NEED TO RECOGNIZE THAT OUR SOCIETAL DRUG PROBLEM CALLS FOR A PROACTIVE APPROACH

Drug addiction is not a criminal problem but a public-health issue. Many of the addicts need mental health support; when we fail to provide it, they turn to drugs. We must recognize that once a person is addicted, their whole life becomes consumed by ensuring they get their next "fix." The solution is not jail, it is treatment.

Recently, I spoke with a judge in London who said that if it wasn't for drug-addict charges and mental health issues appearing in his court, he would have 80 percent more time for serious criminal cases. Considering that incarceration costs on average over one hundred thousand dollars per inmate annually, and keeping in mind the astronomical costs for health care that arise when overdoses occur, the cost to implement a mandatory treatment program would ultimately result in savings.[44] The individual could once again become a contributing member of society. On top of this, we would free up court time, cut down on emergency-room visits and lessen wait times, reduce police response times, and cultivate greater safety in the streets of our city centres.

I realize there is no magic bullet, but the current practices—which do absolutely nothing to minimize the drug epidemic—are a dismal failure.

THE NEED FOR POSITIVE SUPPORT FOR FRONTLINE WORKERS

I really debated about whether to include the next few paragraphs in this book, but as I have tried to be totally factual in this book, I feel that including this is important. I also feel this may help retired or serving members seek support, something I should have done years ago.

I never realized how much my career choices impacted my family, all of whom are precious to me. I have mentioned many times the lack of support throughout my career, not just for me but for any officer suffering from various stressors. In my day, you just did not admit you were suffering, as it was a sign of weakness. I didn't realize the extent of the detrimental effects my career had on me until late 2021. My daughter Nicole wrote a letter for veterans. It initially floored me. But the truth is the truth, and since she works as a mental health support worker, with expertise in her own field, I accepted that she is right, knowing that I have lived on Tylenol with codeine for most of my career.

NIKI'S LETTER

It is devastating to think that so many veterans walk around daily experiencing post-traumatic stress disorder symptoms without seeking any support or assistance. The lack of services is disheartening, and the hoops individuals need to jump through to obtain services and treatment—treatment that should be mandated by their employees, in this case the RCMP, in the first place—is unacceptable.

As a result of the police culture, my father, now sixty-eight years old, has lived with PTSD for over half of his life. He has turned to opioids to cope with depressive symptoms and chronic pain. His central nervous system is frequently heightened, which makes it difficult [for him] to cope with any amount of stress in a healthy manner. The unhealthy cycle further exacerbates his IBS symptoms, which often result in frequent hospital and doctor visits. In addition, he experiences frequent night terrors which lead to unrestful, interrupted sleep, perpetuating the negative impact on his mental and physical health.

It is heartbreaking to watch my father experience a life of pain and to abide by the "I'm fine" police culture. Throughout his career he was taught to sweep his emotions under the rug and move forward with no supports or appropriate debrief sessions when [he and his team] experienced an unimaginable situation. [With this] lack of supports, he instead resorted to unhealthy ways of coping: opioids (legal), immersing himself in work, and isolating from people he cared about.

I commend my father for his resilience, as often the outcome in this situation is homelessness and heavy substance use, *and* his resilience does not dispute the pain he experienced over the years. The trauma he has endured and continues to live with should never be experienced by anyone. I recognize seeking support for an illness someone has lived with for much of their life is not an easy feat and therefore, needs to be handled effectively, timely, and compassionately.

Chapter Twenty-Five

LOOKING TO THE FUTURE

At the end of January 2023, I was contacted by CTV's *W5* and asked to comment on the Pivot Airlines drug-importation fiasco.[45] I was furnished with Eric Szeto's and Avery Haines's investigative findings. They presented several issues that raised considerable red flags on the file's handling.

Allegedly the RCMP had been aware of the importation well before the seizure in the Dominican. The drugs were hidden in the aviation (electronics) bay, which, according to *W5* pilot sources, could have put the flight at risk. If the RCMP had been aware, why let the crew languish after the seizure? *W5*'s investigation showed that several of the passengers, the majority of whom were from Alberta, had previous drug records. Rahul Nanda, the lawyer, represented all the passengers. Meanwhile, Nanda's brother is known to law enforcement as a possible drug dealer.

Years ago, RCMP investigators would have been all over this case. But the RCMP liaison officer for the Dominican region appears to have been an absentee landlord. At the time of my interview, *W5* learned that investigators were beginning to ask questions. One must realize that the seizure of the drugs allegedly destined for Canada established grounds for a conspiracy-to-import investigation. Due to the amounts involved, and the past criminal records of many of the players, it stands to reason that this should have been jumped on at the outset; if the RCMP were aware of the importation, why had action not been taken?

The crew deserve answers. Why does it take journalists to shed light on cases that should have been reported as police investigations? We know that our government has signed an immigration agreement with the Dominican Republic, as this is a popular Canadian holiday destination. The question to be asked is this: Does an agreement trump a clear case of corruption? *W5* showed, on camera, Dominican officials loading the cocaine in the aviation bay.

What with China, Russia, cybercrime, and the opioid epidemic, have future Canadians been left vulnerable?

While working with *W5*, another story came to light that calls into question our justice system and Canada's ability to tackle organized crime. In Alberta, Gursharanjit Parmar, Joshua Okabe, and Ricco King had their drug-importation charges dropped. Also included in the dropped charges was a murder charge, wherein Jason Antonio, thirty-nine years old, died in a northeast Calgary shooting in October 2014. He had been charged the year before when police seized more than one million dollars' worth of methamphetamine, cocaine, and crack cocaine.[46] This was a firm example of case law superseding the need for justice in serious criminal cases, based on the argument that the accused did not get a speedy trial. What about the individuals he trafficked to, those who became addicted, and some of whom likely overdosed. Where's their justice?

Jordan case law demands the right to a trial without excessive delays. The concept itself is reasonable, but organized-crime cases are complex and often cannot move forward as quickly as one would like. The Supreme Court ignores this with its new defined timelines, resulting in organized criminals walking free. This case—the one where Antonio's murderers walked free—highlights the issues at hand. It is questionable as well that the charges were dropped due to a decision of the lower court being delayed.

I would submit that the average person, if given the chance, would disagree that a delay should enable organized criminals to avoid prosecution. For years, courts have used the concept of "bringing of justice into disrepute" as a factor when assessing law enforcement's actions. My question is, what about the justice system? Surely delays in complex and grievously serious criminal offences should not result in cases being thrown out. What about the victims and their families? Is this really justice—or is it bringing the system into disrepute?

Just after completing the interview with *W5*, I was approached by CBC reporter Ashley Burke, who was working on a story involving Canadian Iranians indicted in the US for violating Iranian sanctions. I was asked to review the indictment and comment on what it meant for Canada.

What was interesting about this story was that it seemed to substantiate the intelligence that the Iranian regime relied on well-placed Iranian citizens in foreign countries to assist it in financing its operations. The Iranian regime—and this is no secret—has been under a multitude of sanctions whose goal it is to rein in the regime and make it more accountable.

Following grand-jury hearings in the case provided by the US district court in California, a number of Iranian individuals were indicted on a total of forty-seven charges, from circumventing sanctions to shipping oil. Strong links were alleged between the Iranian regime and the Canadian Iranians domiciled in Toronto. The indictment also alleged the individuals evaded US sanctions against Iran by disguising US fund transfers on behalf of Iranian oil companies through front companies outside of Iran; they had created fraudulent documents "proving" that the US dollar transactions did not involve Iran.

Those same individuals had mortgage and development companies in Canada, perfect vehicles to launder money. Following the indictment, the principals transferred the residential and corporate interests into their wives' names, which is a typical nominee money-laundering tactic. Massive amounts of money (in the tens of millions) had allegedly been moved by the indicted.

Transnational criminals and kleptocrats continue to use Canada as a safe haven. The ongoing media attention on our flimsy enforcement-and-prosecution structure makes us an attractive location from which to operate and launder.

I'd like to share a quote from the Mass Casualty Commission, which reviewed one of the worst shooting tragedies in Canadian history.

> The long-anticipated Mass Casualty Commission's final report into the 2020 Nova Scotia shooting highlighted significant systemic issues within Canada's national police force and called for widespread changes.[47]

These words, too, from the report *Turning the Tide Together*: "The future of the RCMP and of provincial policing requires focused re-evaluation. . . . We need to rethink the role of the police in a wider ecosystem of public safety."[48]

And as Commissioner Leanne Fitch said, "Significant changes are needed to address various community-safety and well-being needs of the twenty-first century."[49]

These findings are commensurate with what I have, for decades, been advocating for. Canada deserves better, and no organization can be expected to be all things to all people. Returning contract policing to the provinces and municipalities would pave the way for the formation of an effective and efficient federal force tasked with investigating organized criminal groups and financial crime, along with terrorist organizations. In this way, expertise would be nurtured and valued.

We owe it to our children and their children to get our heads out of the sand and ensure our politicians focus on the real issues affecting this country. Transnational organized crime is carefully orchestrated. Rogue governments may be driven by goals that don't necessarily serve their population, and sadly, far too many democratic governments have lost sight of what is really important, continually focusing on special-interest issues rather than on issues that trouble the whole of our country.

Most recently we have been subjected to China's increasing entrenchment in Canada. Not only has China influenced our governments, but Chinese Canadians have been made susceptible to China's domineering influence. We continue to witness a government that, in my view, has totally lost touch with what is occurring in Canadian society and heedlessly goes along with policies that cater to the "hot topic" special interests of vocal minorities.

We continue to see the erosion of our military—inadequacies in skill level, equipment, and recruitment—even while our military leaders issue dire warnings on the state of its readiness. Our government is focused more on a gun buy-back program than it is on dealing with the real issues of rampant drug use, an inadequate bail system, and the assault on law enforcement by dissatisfied citizens.

In a recently publicized speech by Vice Admiral Mark Norman, he stated:

> I genuinely believe that the global security situation has fundamentally changed in the past few years, and the complacency and attendant 'risk management' approaches to defence and security matters implemented by successive governments— of all political orientations—have severely under-

mined not only our credibility as a nation but, more importantly, our national security.

When we consider Norman's words in the context of Chinese police stations and their "Belt and Road Initiative," it should be an alarming wake-up call for Western governments and more so for Canada. Norman concluded:

> Finally, the politicization of security and defence is irresponsible, dangerous, and must stop immediately. These vital national interests are too important to be subject to the whims of short-term political interests and public opinion.[50]

I hope to live long enough to see some of my suggestions embraced by our government and that the respective agencies take this seriously enough to start taking action toward transformation. The current changes occurring in British Columbia flowing from the Cullen Commission (i.e., unexplained-wealth orders and a sustained investment in policing and prosecution) will, I hope, inspire the other provinces and the federal government to follow suit.

The time for studying the problem has long passed. We know the problem and we know how to fix some of it.

Two quotes sum up my thoughts. The first is from Edmund Burke: "The only thing necessary for the triumph of evil is for good [people] to do nothing." The second is from Robert Kennedy: "Every society gets the kind of criminal it deserves. What is equally true is that every community gets the kind of law enforcement it insists on."

It is decision time for Canada. If not now, when?

Photos

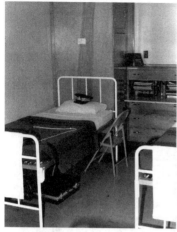

ABOVE: Depot (Regina) training

RIGHT: Off to Montreal for Undercover training

BELOW: Back to Langley and place in uniform notwithstanding long hair

1976 Toronto Undercover assignment where I first met Pat Kelly

EX-MOUNTIE'S WIFE PLUNGED TO DEATH

On March 29, 1981, Jeanette Kelly plunged to her death from the 17th floor of her luxurious Palace Pier apartment overlooking Lake Ontario. Two years later, her husband Patrick, a former RCMP undercover officer, was charged with her murder. In the first of a five-part series, Max Haines recounts the story of the Kellys' lives together, culminating with Jeanette's death and with Patrick standing trial for her murder.

MAX HAINES Crime Flashback

When Pat Kelly was still a child, his family moved from Toronto to Victoria, B.C. He attended school in Victoria, graduating from Mountain View High School after completing Grade 12.

Pat Kelly, a clean-cut, bright young man, tried his hand at banking. He obtained employment with the Bank of Montreal in Port Alberni, B.C., and was soon transferred to Dawson Creek. It was only a matter of a few months before Pat knew that the regimented life of a banker was not for him. He left the bank and caught on with a logging company, but here too, a restless streak, maybe an adventurous one, made Pat look to greener pastures. What could hold more promise of adventure than the RCMP?

On Nov. 3, 1970, Pat Kelly joined the Mounties and was assigned to Regina for basic training. Six months later he graduated and was sent to Toronto, where he spent four months on duty at Pearson International Airport. Next step in Pat's law enforcement career found him stationed at the RCMP detachment at Owen Sound. Here he obtained his first taste of undercover work, becoming involved in drugs and customs investigations.

A year later, he was transferred back to Toronto to enroll in a French course, which lasted 18 months. Pat was then assigned to the drug squad. Soon he was an undercover drug squad operator.

In 1974, Pat's superiors sent him to the University of Javeria in Bogota, Colombia, to take part in a total immersion course in Spanish. Later, while vacationing in Acapulco with fellow RCMP officer Wayne Humby, Pat met his future wife, Jeanette Hanlon.

The daughter of an automobile dealer in Glasgow, Scotland, attractive Jeanette hit it off with Pat right from the start. She was an employee of Avianca, Colombia's national airline, and was stopping over in Acapulco on her way back to Scotland after setting up a computer program for an airline in New Zealand. Jeanette and Pat were seldom apart during the week they spent in Mexico.

Jeanette, who had a full airline pass, continued on to Scotland to visit her family. She and Pat kept in constant touch by phone for a few weeks. Then she joined him in Toronto. The lovers discussed marriage. Jeanette was smitten. She returned to Scotland, but three months later emigrated to Canada to live with Pat Kelly. Ten months after her return, on Sept. 30, 1975, Jeanette and Pat were married.

They had become good friends with another couple, Dawn Tabor and John Pinkerton Hastey, better known as Pinky. The pair had been childhood friends in Maine. A short time after they arrived in Toronto, Dawn and Pinky married. They lived at 1900 Bloor St. E. in Mississauga. Pat and Jeanette lived at Applewood Towers in Mississauga. Dawn Hastey is a name to remember. Sometime

later, in the tangled web of the Kellys' life, Dawn would play a starring role.

In 1976, Pat and Jeanette purchased their first home from Pat's cousin, Jack McKay, at 14 George St. in Cookstown, north of Metro. Jeanette discovered she had a flair for interior decorating. The young couple worked several months renovating their new home.

Once they were nicely settled, Jeanette opened a craft shop specializing in homemade quilts. She named it The Quilt Shop. Farmers' wives around Cookstown brought their homemade quilts to Jeanette, who sold them at a profit. The trendy shop gradually caught on. While it didn't produce a large profit, it did pay its own way. In the summer of 1978, the Kellys sold their shop at a small profit.

That summer of 1978, Pat was deeply

involved in an RCMP undercover drug operation. It was a rather stressful time for Pat. He had been attempting to sell his home in Cookstown and purchase a condominium in the Palace Pier apartment building in the west end of Toronto. The house in Cookstown had been up for sale with no takers for over 18 months. This was of some concern, since Pat had put $3,000 down on the new apartment, but required a further $5,700 to close the deal toward the total price of $87,000.

Later, Pat would testify that he had several sources from whom he could have borrowed the balance of his down payment. However, all his problems appeared to evaporate when, in August, the Cookstown house burned to the ground. At the time of the fire, Pat claimed that he was at a lodge in Algonquin Park, while Jeanette was visiting her family in Glasgow. Pat phoned Jeanette, who flew back to Toronto.

He collected insurance for burned home

Arson was strongly suspected. Jeanette was understandably shocked when Pat was charged with setting fire to the house, along with two counts of attempting to defraud the insurance companies. Their marriage deteriorated into a strained relationship. In Pat's own words, ". . . Basically a platonic relationship took place. I didn't get in her way and she didn't get in mine. We would often socialize together and go to a movie perhaps or go to dinner. It was quite remarkably a congenial atmosphere considering the circumstances."

For some time after the fire, Pat and Jeanette lived at the Holiday Inn in Don Mills under police protection. The drug probe involving Pat had been finalized in July and the fire had taken place in August. There was a grave suspicion that Pat's life was in danger. To this day, Pat claims that criminals burned his house shortly after his cover was blown.

Others obviously had a different theory, but things took a turn for the better for the Kellys. Pat was discharged on the arson charges. He collected $60,000 in insurance for the house and $55,000 for contents, in all $115,000.

Pat and Jeanette took a holiday in Mexico. The Kellys grew much closer now that the terrible possibility of a conviction and prison sentence had been lifted from their shoulders. When they returned to Toronto, there seemed little reason not to move into the Palace Pier.

On Oct. 3, 1978, the Kellys moved into their luxurious new apartment.

Part 2 next week . . .

Death at Palace Pier

Ex-Mountie undercover officer Patrick Kelly (above) and wife Jeanette (below) lived in a 17th-floor condominium at the Palace Pier (right) when she fell to her death in 1981 (dotted line).

DRUGS SEIZED in a series of raids that began at daybreak today are displayed by Sgt. Wayne Horrocks of the Royal Canadian Mounted Police at a press confer- ence at RCMP headquarters. The drugs, including heroin, cocaine, opium and hashish, were mailed into Canada from Far East. Eighty-four have been charged.

—Star photo by Bob Olsen

Drugs by mail, 84 charged

Continued from page 1

i n g charges. Sgt. John McDonnell of the narcotics squad said today that only three of the 56 arrested in May have been charged in today's round-up.

Venner said the mailing of narcotics began about a year ago to bypass increased scrutiny of persons suspected of arriving in Canada with drugs.

He said that one group of traffickers set up a system of sending a man to Bangkok, Thailand, and to Hong Kong to arrange the mass first-class mail delivery of narcotics.

To avoid suspicion, the far eastern contact man was changed frequently.

Venner said heroin, cocaine, opium and hashish "worth well over a million dollars on the illicit market" was purchased by six undercover officers of the three forces during t h e year-long investigation.

The RCMP officer said the investigation was costly because the RCMP had to supply large sums of money to make purchases — the largest being a $25,000 buy of cocaine. He said this money was recovered when a suspected seller was arrested.

Undercover officers infiltrated southern Ontario's d r u g subculture making buys of a large variety of drugs.

"The targets were traffickers at a high level, many of them importers with their own network of distributors," V e n n e r added.

Venner said that 30 officers from the three forces combined for the first time in the investigation and 75 more were assigned to arresting suspects today.

The Post Office Act severely handicaps police in curtailing drug trafficking by mail, Venner commented. He said post office investigators are trying to circumvent regulations to allow police to examine mail suspected of containing drugs.

Most of the heroin reaching Metro is being shipped from the Far East and "not the traditional markets in Europe," Venner added.

"What we very badly need, quite frankly, is a search provision clause for first-class mail on reasonable and probable grounds," Venner said.

He said the recent separate round-up of traffickers by the three police forces in Metro is a good sign that "we've turned the corner" in t h e drug enforcement field.

Vancouver undercover
assignment into
organized crime, 1980

45 charged with drug trafficking

Province News Services

Another roundup of suspected heroin and cocaine traffickers has been launched in the Vancouver area with 67 drug trafficking charges being laid against 45 people. Underground operations over the last six months were aimed primarily at suspected suppliers and importers. Police said some of those sought are believed to have been in the business for as long as 20 years.

Death threats take toll on drug agents

BY PETER MOON
The Globe and Mail

*Stress of murder contracts
problem for undercover men*

Undercover assignment into the Miller smuggling organization, 1996

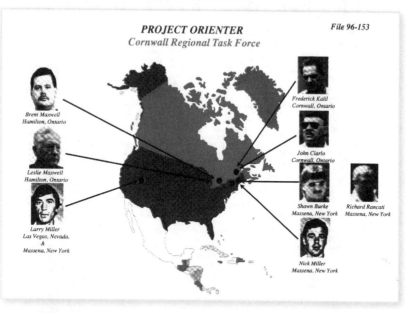

PROJECT ORIENTER
Cornwall Regional Task Force

File 96-153

Brent Maxwell
Hamilton, Ontario

Leslie Maxwell
Hamilton, Ontario

Larry Miller
Las Vegas, Nevada.
&
Massena, New York

Frederick Kalil
Cornwall, Ontario

John Ciarlo
Cornwall, Ontario

Shawn Burke
Massena, New York

Richard Rancati
Massena, New York

Nick Miller
Massena, New York

Top smugglers nabbed, police say

Illegal liquor operation may have cost Canada up to $2 million in taxes

By Don Campbell
Citizen police reporter

Police have charged 12 people and are searching for one more after breaking up a massive operation that smuggled illegal liquor from the United States into Canada.

The charges came after a 10-month undercover operation involving the RCMP, Ontario Provincial Police, Cornwall police and Canada Customs, working in a group called the Cornwall Regional Task Force. They had help from the FBI, the U.S. Bureau of Alcohol, Tobacco and Firearms and the Internal Revenue Service, U.S. Customs and the U.S. Border Patrol.

"We have nailed the highest profile group of people since the inception of the task force," said OPP Det. Sgt. Denis Girard, a lead investigator with the Task Force, said Friday.

"We're talking the top top-level, high-echelon people in the organization. We've had good success nailing the lower-level smugglers. This time we got the top guys."

The smugglers, operating out of Massena, New York, allegedly defrauded the Canadian government of almost $2 million in taxes over the summer by bringing illegal alcohol across the Canada-U.S. border to buyers in Southern Ontario.

The gang reportedly bought large quantities of alcohol from U.S. distillers, moved it to points near the border using legitimate trucking firms, then used Detroit-Windsor border crossings to bring it to Canada in tractor trailers. The alcohol allegedly was taken to waiting purchasers in the Hamilton area.

Police disguised as truck drivers willing to cross the border with illegal cargoes infiltrated the ring. This allowed authorities to seize two tractor trailers containing $1 million worth of liquor — mostly whisky, vodka and gin — and about $400,000 in cash.

Drugs, firearms seized

Drugs and firearms were also seized during a series on raids in Massena, and the Ontario cities of Cornwall, Hamilton and Niagara Falls.

Twelve people — two from Cornwall, four from Massena and others from the Hamilton area — face a total of 350 charges, ranging from conspiracy to possess illegal liquor to defrauding the Canadian and Ontario governments.

Police have also issued a Canada-wide warrant for Massena nightclub owner Larry Miller. The owner of Club 37 in Massena, is thought to be on the run in Russia, according to police.

Though the undercover operation lasted 10 months, the investigators keyed in on a three-month period where, by police estimates, the ring netted a profit of $1.1 million.

Once agents infiltrated the ranks, acting as the carriers of the illegal goods, the operation was allowed to continue under police surveillance.

Nine fully-loaded tractor trailers were allowed to cross the border into Canada as police gathered evidence.

The police operation culminated Wednesday in a series of raids across the province. Some 50 U.S. federal agents from several agencies searched seven buildings in the Massena area.

Police were upbeat, but were careful when gauging how big a chunk they had taken out of the smuggling business in the Cornwall area.

"What we're happy about is this was in no way Akwesasne-related," said Girard, referring to the Mohawk reservation that straddles the Ontario, Quebec and New York borders. It has long been a conduit for smuggled goods such as tobacco and alcohol.

"These were organized crime types."

FACING PAGE, TOP: Bus Hijacking Parliament Hill

FACING PAGE, BOTTOM: Media on the ultimate arrest of Handlen

HIJACK DRAMA
Surrender ends eight-hour hostage ordeal

By Greg Weston
and Tonda MacCharles

A nightmare for 11 people taken hostage aboard a New York-bound Greyhound bus ended peacefully at dusk on Parliament Hill Friday when the armed hijacker surrendered to police.

RCMP have arrested, but not charged, a man who identified himself as 38-year-old Charles Yacoub, said deputy commissioner Gilles Favreau.

Yacoub is to appear in provincial court today to be charged, his lawyer Gilles Charlebois said.

Yacoub claimed to represent a group called the Liberation Front for Christian Lebanon. But police said "as far as we know" no such group exists.

Three shots were fired from the bus during the eight-hour ordeal but no one was hurt.

RCMP say Yacoub is believed to have entered Canada from Lebanon in 1974, but Favreau would not confirm the man's citizenship. Yacoub has a minor criminal record, with one "unrelated" conviction, he said.

During tense negotiations with RCMP Sgt. Gary Clements and Ottawa lawyer Alain Theoret, Yacoub spoke "calmly" in both English and French.

Police would not confirm the demands the hijacker made in two communiqués. He reportedly wanted the withdrawal of Syrian troops from Lebanon and the release of Lebanese prisoners in Syria.

They were demands the Canadian government could not possibly have "done anything about," said Favreau.

The hijacker told police at one point that he would blow up the vehicle with dynamite unless his demands were met.

Heavily armed police sniper units sealed off the Hill throughout the afternoon and kept the bus cornered on the front lawn of the Parliament Buildings. Police also evacuated the main Parliament Buildings and those across Wellington Street.

The drama began at 11:45 a.m. when Greyhound bus No. 1482 headed for New York City pulled out of downtown Montreal terminal with 11 passengers on board.

Twenty minutes later, the bus passed through the tollgate at the Champlain bridge over the St. Lawrence River, just south of

Please see HIJACK/A2

Freed passengers stand against bus to be checked for weapons while police hold suspect on the ground

Wayward bus: how the police lost track

The Canadian Press

Police were taken by surprise when a hijacked bus carrying hostages arrived on Parliament Hill Friday afternoon, even though the bus had been seized two hours earlier in Montreal.

Neither Ottawa police nor the RCMP security detachment on Parliament Hill had any warning that a hijacked bus was heading their way, police confirmed Friday night, apparently because they assumed it was headed elsewhere.

"Absolutely not," was the answer given by a police spokesman when asked whether any prior warning had been received.

Even hours after the hostage-taking was over, senior RCMP officials were unable to explain how the bus ended its way between two of Canada's biggest cities, on

a busy highway, without being detected.

The Greyhound bus was seized on the Champlain Bridge, a major connection for roads heading south from the island of Montreal.

A hostage was released at the bridge, who informed authorities at a toll booth that the hijacking was under way.

Quebec provincial police set up roadblocks at strategic points, dispatched a helicopter and patrol cars, but the big red-white-and-blue intercity bus evaded them all.

"We had no way of knowing it was going to Ottawa," said one Quebec provincial police spokesman.

A spokesman for the RCMP in Ottawa, Cpl. Pierre Belanger, confirmed to reporters that local

Please see BUS/A23

Hostages watch police frisk suspect after surrender

THE FULL STORY

- **HOSTAGE CIRCUS:** Drama draws crowd/F1
- **NICHOLS:** An eyewitness account/F1
- **LEVEL-HEADED:** Bus driver earns praise/F2
- **BUS SAFETY:** No plans for tighter security/F2
- **TEAMWORK:** Police worry ready/F3
- **TIME:** Negotiator's best friend/F3

Garry Taylor Handlen, accused child killer, evaded charges for 39 years

Suspect in B.C. child killings charged with 1st-degree murder in deaths of 2 girls

Greg Rasmussen · CBC News · Posted: Dec 02, 2014 4:08 PM EST | Last Updated: December 2, 2014

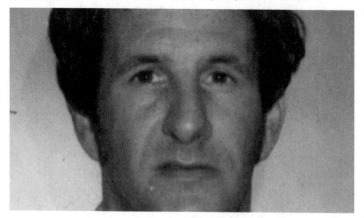

Police want to speak with anyone who remembers Garry Taylor Handlen, pictured here in the '70s. He is accused of killing 11-year-old Kathryn-Mary Herbert and 12-year-old Monica Jack. (RCMP)

Acknowledgements

I am deeply indebted to the many colleagues who worked with me in my investigative units, many of whom I consider friends.

I also want to acknowledge my editors. Because of you, I can say that what has been finalized is transformative and worthy of publishing.

I am also in awe of the generous and humbling comments made by Jeffrey Robinson, Declan Hill, and Christian Leuprecht, all individuals I have known for many years and whom I have the highest of respect for.

Lastly, I acknowledge the tremendous support of Dean Baxendale, who has believed in me and my story since the beginning. I will be forever indebted.

About the Author

Garry Clement has thirty-four years of policing experience. An expert and advocate for financial-crime prevention, he has worked as the national director for the RCMP's Proceeds of Crime program and as an investigator and undercover operator in some of the highest organized-crime levels throughout Canada. During Garry's policing career, he received numerous awards and commendations for his investigative abilities, inclusive of recognitions from the US Drug Enforcement Administration and the CIA.

Garry began working in the anti–money laundering arena in 1983, and was one of the pioneers of the RCMP's Proceeds of Crime program. Since 2007 he has worked as a consultant with a focus on financial crime and independent money-laundering reviews for the money-service business industry, credit unions, and securities firms. Today, he is the chief anti–money laundering officer for VersaBank.

Endnotes

INTRODUCTION

1. Denise Ryan, "Diversion of Vancouver's 'Safer Supply': Growing Problem or Urban Myth?" *Vancouver Sun*, May 28, 2023, https://vancouversun. com/news/local-news/safe-supply-hydromorphone-diversion-is- being-monitored#:~:text=In%20April%2C%20B.C.%20Chief%20 Coroner,death%2C%20is%20an%20urban%20myth.

2. David Cassels, "Reboot the Police. They Can Serve Communities Better," *Ottawa Citizen*, July 24, 2020, https://ottawacitizen.com/opinion/cassels- reboot-the-police-they-can-serve-communities-better.

PART I: YOUNG GARRY

3. "History of the Divisions," Royal Canadian Mounted Police (website), last modified March 8, 2023, https://www.rcmp-grc.gc.ca/corporate- organisation/history-histoire/history-divisions-histoire-divisions-eng.htm.

PART II: THE BEGINNING OF UNDERCOVER

4. Ed Conroy, "Toronto's Last Grindhouse Rises Again," *Blog TO*, March 13, 2015, https://www.blogto.com/film/2015/03/torontos_last_ grindhouse_rises_again/.

PART III: VANCOUVER DRUGS

5. "Tommy Chong Remembers Vancouver Drug Squad Officer Abe Snidanko, 'The Narc of Narcs,'" *CBC Radio: As It Happens*, August 11, 2017, https://www.cbc.ca/radio/asithappens/as-it-happens-thursday-

edition-1.4241899/tommy-chong-remembers-vancouver-drug-squad-officer-abe-snidanko-the-narc-of-the-narcs-1.4241904.

6.   "Penthouse Nightclub Founder Murdered Thirty Years Ago," *City News*, September 17, 2023, https://vancouver.citynews.ca/2013/09/17/penthouse-nightclub-founder-murdered-30-years-ago/.

PART IV: STARTING AT HEADQUARTERS

7.   David Pugliese, "1985 Terrorist Attack on Ottawa Embassy Remembered," *Ottawa Citizen*, March 11, 2015, https://ottawacitizen.com/news/national/defence-watch/1985-terrorist-attack-on-ottawa-embassy-remembered.

8.   Samantha Wright Allen, "Justice Remains 'Undone' in Ottawa Slaying of Turkish Diplomat," *Ottawa Citizen*, August 27, 2014, https://ottawacitizen.com/news/local-news/justice-remains-undone-in-ottawa-slaying-of-turkish-diplomat.

9.   *Liaison*, vol. 12, no. 8, September 1986, archive published by Public Safety Canada, https://www.publicsafety.gc.ca/lbrr/archives/liaison%2012-8-1986.pdf.

10.   Tom Blickman, "Rothschilds of the Mafia in Aruba," *Transnational Organized Crime*, vol. 3, no. 2, May 29, 1997, https://www.tni.org/en/publication/the-rothschilds-of-the-mafia-on-aruba#:~:text=According%20to%20Natoli%2C%20%22the%20clan,the%20nucleus%20of%20the%20clan.

11.   Kelly Egan, "Still 'Scarred' Thirty Years Later, Death Comes to Driver of Hill's Hijacked Bus," *Ottawa Citizen*, June 20, 2018, https://ottawacitizen.com/opinion/columnists/egan-still-scarred-30-years-later-death-comes-to-driver-of-hills-hijacked-bus.

PART V: MID-CAREER

12.   Paul Cherry, "Power, Corruption, and Cocaine: The Story Behind a Scandal that Rocked the RCMP," *Montreal Gazette*, December 17, 2022, https://montrealgazette.com/news/local-news/details-behind-why-a-corrupt-high-ranking-mountie-took-his-own-life-30-years-ago.

13.   "Merchant Chooses to Return for Trial," *South China Morning Post*, September 17, 1993, https://www.google.com/search?client=safari&rls=en&q=sent+via+airmail+from+bangkok+to+vancouver+roger+mcmeans&ie=UTF-8&oe=UTF-8.

14. Central Intelligence Agency, "Central Intelligence Agency (CIA) Freedom of Information Act (FOIA) Case Log October 2000– April 2002," *Government Attic*, February 8, 2021, https://www. governmentattic.org/39docs/CIAfoiaCaseLog_Oct_2000-Apr_2002.pdf.

15. "Paul Desmarais Remembered as Visionary Entrepreneur with Great Influence," *CBC News*, October 9, 2013, https://www.cbc.ca/news/ business/paul-desmarais-remembered-as-visionary-entrepreneur-with-great-influence-1.1931144.

16. *Commission of Inquiry into Money Laundering in British Columbia* (website), last modified June 3, 2022, https://www.cullencommission.ca.

17. Barry Ellsworth, "Canada's National Police Force Shuts Down 'Chinese Police Stations,'" *Anadolu Agency*, February 6, 2023, https://www.aa.com. tr/en/americas/canada-s-national-police-force-shuts-down-chinese-police-stations-/2912358#:~:text=Police%20in%20Canada%20said%20 Thursday,Canadian%20Mounted%20Police%20(RCMP).

18. "Belt and Road Initiative," *The World Bank*, March 29, 2018, https://www. worldbank.org/en/topic/regional-integration/brief/belt-and-road-initiative.

19. Ronald T.P. Alcala, Eugene (John) Gregory, and Shane Reeves, "China and the Rule of Law: A Cautionary Tale for the International Community, *Just Security*, June 28, 2018, https://www.justsecurity. org/58544/china-rule-law-cautionary-tale-international-community/.

PART VI: ON MY WAY OUT

20. Commission of Inquiry into the Actions of Canadian Officials in Relation to Maher Arer, "Arar Commission: About the Inquiry," *Library and Archives Canada*, last modified July 5, 2005, https://epe.lac-bac. gc.ca/100/206/301/pco-bcp/commissions/maher_arar/05-07-09/www. ararcommission.ca/eng/index.htm.

21. Francine Bastien, "Arar Commission Releases Its Findings on the Handling of the Maher Arar Case," *Government of Canada*, September 18, 2006, https://www.canada.ca/en/news/archive/2006/09/arar-commission-releases-findings-handling-maher-arar-case.html.

22. Commission of Inquiry into the Actions of Canadian Officials in Relation to Maher Arer, "Arar Commission Releases Its Findings on the Handling of the Maher Arar Case," *Library and Archives Canada*, September 18, 2006, https://epe.lac-bac.gc.ca/100/206/301/pco-bcp/ commissions/maher_arar/06-12-13/www.ararcommission.ca/eng/ ReleaseFinal_Sept18.pdf.

23. The Honourable Frank Iacobucci, "Internal Inquiry into the Actions of Canadian Officials in Relation to Abdullah Almalki, Ahmad Abou El Maati, and Muayyed Nureddin: Supplement to Public Report," *Amnesty International*, 2010, https://www.amnesty.ca/sites/amnesty/files/imce/images/Iacobucci%20Inquiry%20Report%20-%20Supplement.pdf.

24. "US Rendition Practice Since 9/11," *Human Rights Watch*, last modified June 2005, https://www.hrw.org/legacy/backgrounder/eca/canada/arar/3.htm.

25. *Extraordinary Rendition, Extraterritorial Detention, and Treatment of Detainees: Restoring Our Moral Credibility and Strengthening Our Diplomatic Standing: Hearing before the Committee on Foreign Relations*, 110th Cong. 257, 2007, https://www.govinfo.gov/content/pkg/CHRG-110shrg40379/html/CHRG-110shrg40379.htm.

26. Paul Barnsley, "Government, RCMP Relationship Questioned," *Windspeaker* magazine, vol. 18, no. 11, 2001, Aboriginal Multi-media Society, https://ammsa.com/publications/windspeaker/government-rcmp-relationship-questioned.

27. "Civilian Members," Cobourg Police Service (website), accessed September 16, 2023, https://cobourgpoliceservice.com/civilian-members/#:~:text=What%20started%20as%20a%20"side,is%20expected%20to%20surpass%20%24244%2C000%2C000.00.

28. Christiane Desjardins, "Drogues, Millions, et Divination," *La Presse*, April 5, 2011, https://www.lapresse.ca/actualites/justice-et-faits-divers/201104/04/01-4386508-drogue-millions-et-divination.php.

29. John Ashcroft, "Prepared Remarks of Attorney General John Ashcroft: Indictment of Elias Cobos-Munoz/Operation Busted Manatee Announcement," June 23, 2004, Washington, District of Columbia, Department of Justice, https://www.justice.gov/archive/ag/speeches/2004/ag62304bustedmanatee.htm.

30. Tu Thanh Ha and Julian Sher, "A Crooked Cop, Drug Money, and Diamonds: Action-packed Allegations at at Montreal Trial," *The Globe and Mail*, March 24, 2011, https://www.theglobeandmail.com/news/national/a-crooked-cop-drug-money-and-diamonds-action-packed-allegations-at-montreal-trial/article573925/.

PART VII: WHAT DO WE DO?

31. R. v. Stinchcombe, [1991] 3 SCR 326, CanLII 45 (SCC), https://www.canlii.org/en/ca/scc/doc/1991/1991canlii45/1991canlii45.html.

ENDNOTES

32. Sean Fine, "Criminal Cases in Ontario on Verge of Collapse Owing to Courthouse Chaos," *The Globe and Mail*, September 14, 2023, https://www.theglobeandmail.com/canada/article-criminal-cases-on-verge-of-collapse-owing-to-courthouse-chaos/#:~:text=Under%20the%20Canadian%20Charter%20of,for%20trials%20in%20superior%20court.

33. Peter Bowal and Thomas D. Brierton, "Stinchcombe: Crown Disclosure of Criminal Evidence," *Law Now*, January 2, 2018, https://www.lawnow.org/stinchcombe-and-crown-disclosure-of-criminal-evidence-2/.

34. "Elements of Wire Fraud," United States Code, Title 18, Section 1343, *Justice Manual*, 941, US Department of Justice (website), last modified January 21, 2020, https://www.justice.gov/archives/jm/criminal-resource-manual-941-18-usc-1343-elements-wire-fraud.

35. "Money Laundering and Racketeering (RICO)," Neff & Sedacca Law Offices (website), accessed September 16, 2023, https://neffsedacca.com/practice-areas/money-laundering-and-racketeering-rico/.

36. Federation of Law Societies of Canada (FLSC) v. Canada (Attorney General), [2013] BCCA 147 (CanLII), https://www.canlii.org/en/bc/bcca/doc/2013/2013bcca147/2013bcca147.html.

37. John F. Kennedy, "Speech at the District Attorney's Convention," July 31, 1959, Milwaukee, Wisconsin, John F. Kennedy: Presidential Library and Museum (website), https://www.jfklibrary.org/archives/other-resources/john-f-kennedy-speeches/milwaukee-wi-19590731#:~:text=Organized%20Crime%20in%20Legitimate%20Business&text=I%20am%20not%20talking%20about,number%20of%20legitimate%20business%20enterprises.

38. "SNC-Lavalin, Subsidiaries Charged with Corruption, Fraud in Libyan Business Probe," *CBC News*, February 19, 2015, https://www.cbc.ca/news/business/snc-lavalin-subsidiaries-charged-with-corruption-fraud-in-libyan-business-probe-1.2963025#:~:text=The%20Mounties%20allege%20that%20between,positions%20to%20influence%20government%20decisions.

39. Global Affairs Canada, "Minister Bibeau Meets with Key Humanitarian Partners," *Government of Canada*, December 3, 2015, https://www.canada.ca/en/global-affairs/news/2015/12/minister-bibeau-meets-with-key-humanitarian-partners.html.

40. Monique Scotti, "SNC-Lavalin Illegally Donated Over $117K to Federal Parties: Elections Canada," *Global News*, September 8, 2016, https://globalnews.ca/news/2927286/snc-lavalin-illegally-donated-over-117k-to-federal-parties-elections-canada/.

41. Duncan McCue, "Canada 'Falling Behind' on Fighting Corruption Abroad: Transparency International Director," *CBC Radio: Cross Country Checkup*, February 17, 2019, https://www.cbc.ca/radio/checkup/canada-falling-behind-on-fighting-corruption-abroad-transparency-international-director-1.5022735.

42. "About," *Transparency International* (website), accessed September 16, 2023, https://www.transparency.org/en/about.

43. Sam Cooper, "It's Long Been Known in BC that RCMP Not Investigating Money Laundering, Sources Reiterating," *Global News*, April 10, 2019, https://globalnews.ca/news/5145925/bc-rcmp-not-investigating-money-laundering-sources/#:~:text=In%20a%20March%202019%20report,law%20enforcement%20and%20soft%20laws.

44. "Average Annual Inmate Expenditures for Federal Correction Services in Canada from FY 2010 to FY 2020," *Statista Research Department*, June 5, 2023, https://www.statista.com/statistics/563028/average-annual-inmate-federal-correctional-services-canada/#:~:text=This%20statistic%20shows%20the%20average,inmates%20averaged%20126%2C253%20Canadian%20dollars.

45. Official *W5*, "Cocaine Cargo II: Who Is Behind the Pivot Airlines Drug-Smuggling Plot?" *CTV W5*, March 11, 2023, YouTube video, 22:53, https://www.youtube.com/watch?v=dGpc2DImKYE.

46. Meghan Grant, "Men Charged in Dominican Republic to Calgary Drug Ring Walk Away from Import, Murder Charges," *CBC News*, June 26, 2019, https://www.cbc.ca/news/canada/calgary/okabe-parmar-king-drug-murder-zanoni-antonio-charges-stayed-1.5191130.

47. Mass Casualty Commission (website), accessed September 16, 2023, https://masscasualtycommission.ca.

48. Lois Ann Dort, "MCC Report Recommends Police Reform, Focus on Gender-based Violence Prevention: Local Women's Centre Calls for Stable Funding," *Blue Line* magazine, April 5, 2023, https://www.blueline.ca/mcc-report-recommends-police-reform-focus-on-gender-based-violence-prevention-local-womens-centre-calls-for-stable-funding/.

49. Michael Gorman, "RCMP Pledges to Review NS Mass Shooting Recommendations, Restore Trust in Province," *CBC News*, March 30, 2023, https://www.cbc.ca/news/canada/nova-scotia/rcmp-n-s-mass-casualty-commission-shooting-police-1.6796034.

50. Roy Green, "Canada Not Taking Security 'Seriously Enough,' Former Vice-Admiral Warns," *Global News*, March 11, 2023, https://globalnews.ca/news/9545028/canada-national-security-mark-norman/.